Ancient Chinese Divination

DIMENSIONS OF ASIAN SPIRITUALITY

Shinto: The Way Home
Thomas P. Kabulis

Chan Buddhism
Peter D. Hershock

Korean Spirituality
Don Baker

Ancient Chinese Divination
Stephen L. Field

Ancient Chinese Divination

STEPHEN L. FIELD

Dimensions of Asian Spirituality

UNIVERSITY OF HAWAI‘I PRESS
Honolulu

DIMENSIONS OF ASIAN SPIRITUALITY
Henry Rosemont, Jr., General Editor

This series makes available short but comprehensive works on specific Asian philosophical and religious schools of thought, works focused on a specific region, and works devoted to the full articulation of a concept central to one or more of Asia's spiritual traditions. Series volumes are written by distinguished scholars in the field who not only present their subject matter in historical context for the non-specialist reader but also express their own views of the contemporary spiritual relevance of their subject matter for global citizens of the twenty-first century.

© 2008 University of Hawai'i Press
All rights reserved
Printed in the United States of America
13 12 11 10 09 08   6 5 4 3 2 1

Grateful acknowledgment is made to the authors for permission
to reprint from the following:
"Preamble" in *Sources of Shang History: The Oracle-Bone Inscriptions of Bronze Age China* (University of California Press), copyright © 1978 David N. Keightley.
"Introduction," in *Fortune-Tellers and Philosophers: Divination in Traditional Chinese Society* (Westview Press), copyright © 1991 Richard J. Smith.

Library of Congress Cataloging-in-Publication Data
Field, Stephen.
Ancient Chinese divination / Stephen L. Field.
p. cm. — (Dimensions of Asian spirituality)
Includes bibliographical references and index.
ISBN 978-0-8248-3245-2 (hardcover : alk. paper) —
ISBN 978-0-8248-3276-6 (pbk. : alk. paper)
1. Divination—China.   I. Title.
BF1762.F54 2008
133.30951—dc22
2008012337

University of Hawai'i Press books are printed on acid-free
paper and meet the guidelines for permanence and
durability of the Council on Library Resources.

Designed by Rich Hendel

Printed by The Maple-Vail Book Manufacturing Group

FOR GAIL

Contents

Editor's Preface ix

Acknowledgments xv

Introduction 1

1. Background: Chinese Correlative Cosmology 7
2. The Origin and Evolution of Chinese Divination 21
3. The *Zhouyi,* or *Zhou Changes* 39
4. *Fengshui,* or Tomb and Residential Site Orientation 63
5. Numerology, or Divination by Counting 84
6. Augury, or Divination by Portentous Signs 106
7. Sortilege, or Divination by Choosing from Lots 118

Concluding Remarks 129

Appendix: Chinese Spelling and Pronunciation 131

Further Reading 133

Index 137

Editor's Preface

ABOUT THIS SERIES

The University of Hawai'i Press has long been noted for its scholarly publications in, and commitment to, the field of Asian studies. The Dimensions of Asian Spirituality series was initiated by the Press in keeping with that commitment. It is a most appropriate time for such a series. A number of the world's religions—major and minor—originated in Asia, continue to influence significantly the lives of almost half the world's peoples, and should now be seen as global in scope, reach, and impact, with rich and varied resources for every citizen of the twenty-first century to explore.

Religion is at the heart of every culture. To be sure, the members of every culture have also been influenced by climate, by geology, and by the consequent patterns of economic activity they have developed for the production and distribution of goods. Only a minimal knowledge of physical geography is necessary to understand why African sculptors largely employed wood as their medium, while their Italian Renaissance brethren usually worked with marble. But while necessary for understanding cultures—not least our own—matters of geography and economics will not be sufficient: wood and marble are also found in China, yet Chinese sculptors carved Confucian sages, Daoist immortals, and Buddhist bodhisattvas from their materials, not *chiwaras* or *pietas*.

In the same way, a mosque, synagogue, cathedral, stupa, and pagoda may be equally beautiful, but they are beautiful in different ways, and the differences cannot be accounted for merely on the basis of the materials used in their construction; their beauty, their ability to inspire awe and to invite contemplation, rests largely on the religious view of the world—and the place of human beings in that world—that inspired and is expressed in their architecture. Thus, the spiritual dimensions of a culture are reflected significantly not only in art and architecture, but in music, myths, poetry, rituals, customs, and patterns of social behavior as well. It therefore follows that if we wish to understand why and how members of other cultures live as they do, we must understand the religious beliefs and practices to which they adhere.

In the first instance, such understanding of the "other" leads to tolerance, which is surely a good thing. Much of the pain and suffering in the world today is attributable to intolerance, a fear and hatred of those who look, think, and act differently. But as technological changes in communication, production, and transportation shrink the world, more and more people must confront the fact of human diversity in multiple diverse forms—both between and within nation-states—and hence there is a growing need to go beyond mere tolerance of difference to an appreciation and celebration of it. Tolerance alone cannot contribute substantively to making the world a better—and sustainable—place for human beings to live, the evils attendant on intolerance notwithstanding, and not to be minimized. But in an important sense, mere tolerance is easy because it is passive: I can fully respect your right to believe and worship as you wish, associate with whomever, and say what you will, even as I ignore you. You assuredly have a right to speak but not to make me listen.

Yet for most of us who live in economically developed societies, or are among the affluent in developing nations, tolerance is not enough. Ignoring the poverty, disease, and gross inequalities that afflict fully a third of the human race will only exacerbate, not alleviate, the conditions responsible for the misery that generates the violence becoming ever more commonplace throughout the world.

Some would have us believe that religion is—as it supposedly always has been—the root cause of the violence, and therefore should be done away with. This negative view is reinforced by invoking distorted accounts of the cosmologies of the world's religious heritages, and pointing out that they are incompatible with much that we know of the world today from science.

But religions are not going to go away, nor should they. Those who see only the untoward influences—influences not to be ignored—are taking "a printed bill of fare as the equivalent for a solid meal," to quote William James. Worse than that, to accuse religion as responsible for most of today's violence worldwide is to obscure a far more important root cause: poverty. In this view, the violence will cease only when the more fortunate of the world become active, take up the plight of the less fortunate, and resolve to create and maintain a more just world, requiring a resolve to fully appreciate the co-humanity of everyone, significant differences in religious beliefs and practices notwithstanding.

Such appreciation should not, of course, oblige everyone to endorse *all* the beliefs and practices followed by adherents of other religions; after all, one may object to certain beliefs and practices within one's own faith. A growing number of Catholics, for instance, support a married clergy, the ordination of women, recognition of rights for gays and lesbians, and full reproductive rights for women. Yet they remain Catholics, believing that the tenets of their faith have the conceptual resources to bring about and justify these changes. In the same way, we can also believe—as a number of Muslim women do—that the Qu'ran and other Islamic theological writings contain the conceptual resources to overcome the inferior status of women in some Muslim countries. And indeed we can believe that every spiritual tradition has within it the resources to counter older practices inimical to the full flourishing of all the faithful—and of the faithful of other traditions as well.

Another reason to go beyond mere tolerance to appreciation and celebration of the many and varied forms of spiritual expression is virtually a truism: the more we look through a window on another culture's beliefs and practices, the more it becomes a mirror of our own (even for those who follow no religious tradition). We must look very carefully and charitably, however, else the reflections become distorted. When studying other religions, most people are strongly inclined to focus on cosmological and ontological questions, asking, What do these people believe about how the world came to be, how it is, and where it is heading? Do they believe in ghosts? Immortal souls? A creator god?

Answering these and related metaphysical questions is of course necessary for understanding and appreciating fully the specific forms and content of the art, music, architecture, rituals, and traditions inspired by the specific religion under study. But the sensitive—and sensible—student will bracket the further question of whether the metaphysical pronouncements are literally true; we must attend carefully to the metaphysics (and theologies) of the religions we study, but questions of their literal truth should be set aside to concentrate on a different question: How could a thoughtful, thoroughly decent human being subscribe to and follow these beliefs and attendant practices?

Studied in this light, we may come to see and appreciate how each religious tradition provides a coherent account of a world not fully amenable to human manipulation, nor, perhaps, even to full human understanding. The metaphysical pronouncements of the world's religions, of course, differ measurably from faith to faith, each of which has had a significant influence on the physical expressions of the respective faith in synagogues, stupas, mosques, pagodas, and cathedrals. Despite these differences among buildings, however, the careful and sensitive observer can see the spiritual dimensions of human life that these sacred structures share and express, and in the same way we can come to see and appreciate the common spiritual dimensions of each religion's differing metaphysics and theology: While the several religious traditions give different answers to the question of the meaning *of* life, they all provide a multiplicity of guidelines and spiritual disciplines to enable everyone to find meaning *in* life, in this world. By plumbing the spiritual depths of other religious traditions, then, we may come to more deeply explore the spiritual resources of our own, and at the same time diminish the otherness of the other and create a more peaceable and just world in which everyone can find meaning in their all-too-human lives.

ABOUT THIS VOLUME

Against this background, we may turn more directly to the fourth offering in the Dimensions of Asian Spirituality series, *Ancient Chinese Divination,* by Stephen L. Field. As China continues to develop into an economic giant and plays an increasingly significant role in world affairs, it will be incumbent on all thoughtful citizens everywhere to learn more about the country and its culture. The present work is an admirable contribution to this effort, for as the author says in his Introduction, "In China, the art of divination had a profound influence on the rise of medicine, science, government, and most importantly, philosophy and religion."

We should not, however, explore the patterns of Chinese divination solely for instrumental reasons, to learn more about the cultural legacy inherited by modern-day Chinese. Rather should we also examine it for its intrinsic interest, and for what it may tell us about our own conceptual framework, including philosophy, religion, and science, no less than for what we learn of the framework within which diviners did their casting in the ancient Middle Kingdom.

The early Chinese studied the natural world less to understand it cognitively—"knowledge for its own sake"—or to manipulate it, but more basically in order to learn how to pattern their personal and societal lives. The person, the state, and the cosmos formed a triad for early Chinese thinkers, and when each part followed its proper path (*dao*) the result was an integrated and harmonious whole. The motions of each one of the three affected significantly the activities of the other two. Their universe "spoke" to the Chinese, telling them (if they listened carefully) what was good and what was not, what made for harmony and what produced cacophony (chaos).

This orientation will seem strange to us, at least initially; we will consider the early Chinese thinkers as either childishly naïve or simply engaged in bad science. This tendency toward dismissal is due to the fact that *our* universe is now silent. Earlier it spoke to our ancestors much as it has to the Chinese, but now it says nothing. The billiard balls, from quanta to quasars, move about in ways that can be made intelligible—at least in the language of mathematics—but they do not speak to us; their motions and patterns cannot have personal or social significance for us because within our present conceptual framework they have no significance whatsoever.

At the heart of the conceptual framework of the ancient Chinese is the *Zhouyi,* or *Zhou Changes,* parts of which probably date from the eleventh century BCE. It is equally a book of divination and cosmology, and more folklore is tied to this book, probably, than to any other Chinese text past or present. It was (and is) employed not only to enable its users to situate themselves with respect to the movements of the heavenly, earthly, and political bodies but also assist in almost everything from selecting auspicious days for weddings, to locating appropriate burial places for ancestors, to choosing fitting names for newborn children. Even *fengshui* (siting), currently the most popular form of Chinese divination being studied and practiced in the West, owes much to the *Zhouyi*. And so do all other types of ancient Chinese divination, as Stephen Field demonstrates when he describes with uncommon clarity other methods of divination, such as numerology, augury, and sortilege, the details of which are relatively unknown even to most scholars with sinological training.

The patterns of belief common to all these forms are not, however, of divinatory import only, nor are they just for understanding certain dimensions of Chinese arts and crafts, for these patterns of belief also invest the texts of Confucianism and Daoism, and later permeated the development of Buddhism in China: hence the overall spiritual significance of this book.

Read carefully, and listen; the universe may speak, at least to some of us, once again.

HENRY ROSEMONT, JR.

Acknowledgments

This book was originally conceived in 2003 when Henry Rosemont approached two Trinity University professors attending a conference in memory of the philosopher David Hall. The first scholar was Xing Wen, who has published a monograph and many articles on various aspects of early Chinese divination. I was the second, invited to collaborate with Wen because I am one of the few scholars in the world conducting research on *fengshui,* the most popular form of Chinese divination in the West.

Xing Wen is a world-class expert on excavated silk and bamboo manuscripts. His knowledge of the excavated texts of the *Guicang* and *Zhouyi* is second to none. I never would have undertaken this project had I not been able to count on his expert guidance. Especially on the topics of Neolithic divination and the origin of the earliest divination manuals, to Wen goes credit for the clarity of the depiction of what is to most eyes a fragmented picture at best. It was also Wen who originally conceived of the book's outline and methodology, in particular, categorizing the many different divinatory techniques into three groups. He has drafted a manuscript in Chinese describing the function of these forms of divination, beginning with an enlightening essay on their origin and evolution; I hope and expect that this manuscript will eventually be published in English. Although the very first draft of the current book was a translation of Wen's original manuscript, the resulting book is essentially my work based on my own understanding of the finer points of divination practice. I am grateful to Xing Wen for allowing me to retain some of his ideas and materials. If errors remain, I am, of course, solely to blame.

In every era of human endeavor, there are individuals who step forward to analyze the worldview of a culture with the intent of redefining its vision of itself. Henry Rosemont is such an individual, and his interpretations of Chinese philosophy in particular and his ruminations on classical and modern Chinese culture in general have considerably changed not only the way the West looks at China but also how we look at ourselves. It is Henry who conceived of the Dimensions of Asian Spirituality series so that interested readers across the English-speaking world might gain insight from the religious perspectives of Asian peoples. I would like to thank him for having me contribute to this series so that I may share my own knowledge of Chinese culture with the reading public. Thanks, too, to Henry for his reading of more than one draft of the manuscript, which significantly improved the book's focus, especially between the first and second drafts of the manuscript. I also want to thank the University of Hawaiʻi Press for its commitment to Asian studies and especially for undertaking this new series on Asian religions. Patricia Crosby, executive editor, is to be commended for the care she lavishes on both authors and manuscripts. Next, I would like to thank the most recognized historian of Chinese divination in the West, Richard Smith of Rice University, whose seminal works in the field have always guided my own work in this area. Rich also read more than one draft of the manuscript, and his comments were a great encouragement in the final stages of the writing.

Finally, my greatest debt is to my family. To my parents, who never objected when I made the fateful decision to study Chinese back when doing so must have seemed more like youthful rebellion, my thanks for their unwavering support. To my elder brother, whose lead I followed in the pursuit of knowledge, my thanks for not losing faith in me when our paths diverged. And most of all, thanks to my wife, Gail Reynolds, who has known me since I was ten years old and still manages to love me unconditionally. I dedicate this book to her.

Introduction

Divination is frowned upon in many modern societies. "The Four Olds" movement at the beginning of the Cultural Revolution attempted to eradicate a number of traditional religious practices in China, including fortune-telling and *fengshui*. In the United States, many local jurisdictions have laws that prohibit the business of fortune-telling. Even the belief in divination is not publicly sanctioned in the United States; were it, Nancy Reagan would not have caused a minor scandal when the press revealed that she had consulted an astrologer while planning President Ronald Reagan's schedule. In spite of the fact that the first lady's behavior was perceived by many as scandalous, divining is still widely practiced in the United States. A recent Harris poll discovered that 31 percent of the population believes in astrology, and virtually every major newspaper has a daily horoscope column. Fortune-telling is also a booming business in China today, although any belief system that can be labeled "superstitious" is still officially banned. Chinese fortune-telling is not as popular in the West as horoscopic astrology; however, *fengshui* has spread to every corner of the Western world. It is the popularity of Chinese *fengshui* that makes this book especially timely.

The act of divining, or the need that humans have to seek divine guidance, is no mystery. The mystery is how divination supposedly works. If my task were to scientifically explain the phenomenon, I would have to say that, psychologically speaking, divination is the intentional use of intuition by the fortune-teller. Or I might define it as the unconscious form of thinking—similar to dreaming—that supports the actions of mediums, who must go into a trance before they can intuit their prophecies. Scientists have even posited the existence of an "ideomotor effect" to explain the working of the divining rod and similar tools of the trade. As the reader will see in the following analysis, most methods for casting the *Zhouyi*, or *Zhou Changes*, are based on random number generation. The ancient diviners must have realized that the only way to insure that the king was not skewing the answer to his question was to seek complete randomness in the oracular response.

It is not my task to rationalize the practice of divination. It is enough to know that in China the art of divination had a profound influence on the rise of medicine, science, government, and most importantly, philosophy and religion. Although I cannot discuss the efficacy of divination in this book and will not teach the reader how to conduct divination, I will do my best to explain how divination evolved in Chinese society from the New Stone Age (seventh–second millennium BCE) until the classical period, which ended with the founding of the Qin dynasty in 221 BCE. Archaeological discoveries of the past few decades have made the task of understanding its ancient origins much easier, although some speculation is required in attempting to develop a comprehensive view of the evolution of divination in early China. Once that is done, however, I will be able to describe in great detail some of the many forms of divination that developed directly and indirectly out of the ancient traditions. The reader will then see how the seemingly diverse systems of Chinese divination are organically related, and it will be abundantly clear that divination has been an important feature in traditional Chinese culture from its beginnings down to modern times. It may be useful at this time to point out that Chinese divination, in actual practice, is extraordinarily complex. Since this book is intended as a general overview, much of that complexity has been sacrificed in the interest of succinctness and clarity. Readers with an appetite for more detail are invited to consult the readings listed at the end of the book.

The Chinese word for divination is *zhanbu,* which specifically refers to the oldest verified form of divination, the cracking of oracle bones. The character *bu* is a pictograph of the crack in the bone, and the character *zhan* appends the additional pictograph for "mouth" beneath that of "crack," to imply the action of explaining the significance of the crack. Another term for divination, *suanming,* which may be loosely translated as "fortune-telling," literally means to "calculate the *ming.*" The meaning of *ming* is the key to understanding both terms that describe the act of divination. Originating in Shang dynasty oracle bone texts as the character *ling,* it meant the "command" of Di, the Emperor on High (or high god), or that of lesser spirits (the ancestors), and nature deities. It was Di's command that the king was seeking to know when he had his diviners crack the bone. *Ming* retained the root meaning of *ling* but also gained the "mouth" component. By the Zhou dynasty, the concept had evolved to become *tianming*, or the mandate of *tian* (usually translated as "heaven"). It was heaven's command that a particular king should rule the kingdom. Eventually, the word gained the meaning of "fate" or "destiny" in general, and a person's fated or destined lifespan in particular. So, to calculate a person's *ming* meant to determine how long he would live. *Ming* in the sense of fate, however, was not immutable; otherwise, divination would have been futile, for divination generally supposes that there exists a means whereby one's fate may be known so that one may have some recourse to change it.

Generally speaking, divination is the act of seeking mantic or prophetic information so that good fortune might be welcomed and misfortune avoided. With respect to the sign or omen that contains the mantic information, it can be naturally occurring and therefore passively received, or it may be actively sought and therefore enticed from the spirits. Some naturally occurring signs might be read by anyone ("red sky in morning, sailor's warning"); others required the eye of a trained observer. Some signs appear so violently in nature that they demand explanation. In the Chinese tradition, such anomalies indicated a disturbance of the normal patterns of the cosmos. Examples of such signs are eclipses, comets, earthquakes, and also the appearance of strange creatures such as phoenixes and dragons. To this day, when an earthquake occurs in China, some people believe heaven and earth are responding to a particular human imbalance: that those in power are abusing their positions. This is a remnant of the ancient belief in the mandate of heaven. A passage from the third-century BCE *Annals of Lü Buwei* says, "When heaven sends down disaster or spreads good fortune, someone is always accountable" (bk. 13).

On the other hand, anomalies can also indicate good fortune. Chinese mythology is replete with stories that tell of the birth of prodigies. For example, Hou Ji, or Chief Millet, is the first ancestor of the clan that founded the Zhou dynasty. It is said that his mother walked upon the footprint of a god and became pregnant. Thinking this was a bad omen, she threw the child in the street when it was born. But oxen and horses avoided the baby. Then she placed it on the ice, but birds covered it with their wings. From these auspicious signs she realized the child was divine and therefore raised it. Hou Ji's great-grandson was Chief Liu, who migrated to a new land on the western bank of the Yellow River. We will encounter Chief Liu again in chapter 4.

Some mantic information can be read only by those gifted with certain powers or trained in particular forms of observation. Wind change, cloud patterns, and the flight of birds, for example, were all open to interpretation. The *Annals of Lü Buwei* records this ornithomantic saying: "Just before the time of King Wen, heaven sent a fire-red crow to alight on the altar of Zhou, holding in its beak a cinnabar scroll" (bk. 13). Ancient Chinese astrologers also made predictions based on the heavenly bodies. The altitude of the moon, the color of the sun, and the positions of the planets with regard to the stars were all sources of information about the future. For example, the following prediction is recorded in the Han dynasty *Records of the Grand Historian:* "There will be war if *Huo* [the Fire Star, or Mars] whelms the Horn, and kings will loathe it in the Heart" (chap. 27). The Horn and Heart are two of the twenty-eight constellations of the Chinese zodiac, seven of which formed the great macro-constellation, the Cerulean Dragon.

The most important forms of divination in ancient China were not based on passive observation of the natural world but involved the deliberate search for the answers to particular questions by the production of signs from various sources. These signs, which were equivalent to omens in the natural world, seem quite abstract to the uninitiated observer. The high god Shang Di, ancestral spirits, and various nature deities could all be persuaded to communicate in *xiang* (images) or in *shu* (numbers). These images and numbers could be coaxed from the spirits in various ways, such as by scorching bones and shells to form cracks or by manipulating stalks of plants or stones to form numerical sequences. For the purposes of this book, I will divide Chinese divination into three systems, based on the method by which the sign or omen is read: (1) divination by counting (numerology), (2) divination by interpreting images or signs (augury), and (3) divination by choosing from lots (sortilege), in which practice a predetermined number or image is chosen randomly or otherwise from a series.

The first chapter of this book provides the reader with an overview of the Chinese cosmological worldview as it existed in the Han dynasty (206 BCE–220 CE), that is, after the golden age of philosophy and at the end of the classical period in ancient China. This material is crucial for readers who are new to the study of China. Chapter 2 discusses the origin and development of the two oldest and most influential forms of divination in Chinese culture: pyro-osteomancy, or divination by the scorching of bones and turtle shells, and milfoil stalk-casting. Beginning with new archaeological information showing that the concept of numbers and the belief in a turtle spirit in the Neolithic period were important functions in primitive divination, the chapter concludes with a discussion of the three *Yi*-style books of divination (those that used milfoil stalks for counting). Chapter 3 focuses on the greatest of the three *Yi* divination manuals—the *Zhouyi*, or *Zhou Changes*, and its position within the tradition of Chinese philosophy, religion, and ideology.

The remainder of the book discusses the many forms of divination that developed from the ancient traditions of stalk-counting and crack-reading. Chapter 4 discusses *fengshui*—also known as Chinese geomancy—the art of tomb and residential site selection. In this chapter, I outline the early history of *fengshui* and then present a detailed analysis of both the Form and Compass Schools. Then I explain the most popular form of *fengshui* marketed in the West today and include a comprehensive examination of its inner workings. Chapter 5 discusses numerology, or divination by counting, including *Yi*-style divination using stalks and coins or counting other objects such as bamboo sticks, and the popular numerical fate-calculation systems of Four Pillars and Purple Palace. Chapter 6 discusses augury or divination by portentous signs, including physiognomy, oneiromancy (dream interpretation), and divination by analysis of the several components of a Chinese character. Chapter 7 discusses sortilege or divination by choosing from lots, including hemerology—choosing the proper day, and picking bamboo sticks, such as Patriarch Lü's medicinal lots.

Throughout the work I have liberally quoted from classical Chinese texts directly, not merely as evidence for what I say, but more importantly, for the reader to appreciate the flavor and style of the sources and their content. Unless noted otherwise, all translations are my own. Finally, I have provided an index of proper names and useful terms, including all the concepts and techniques I have discussed in the book. These terms' Chinese transliterations follow in parentheses because I realize that my translations may differ from those of other writers.

CHAPTER 1

Background
Chinese Correlative Cosmology

Early Chinese cosmology, like many primitive cosmologies, was essentially a correlative thought system that sought to organize the observable world into categories whose meaning derived from their association with one another. Consequently, one of the most important associations was that between the human being and the universe. Unlike some civilizations, China, as seen through the earliest Chinese texts, had no story of creation, intentional or otherwise; such myths came in the waning days of the golden age of philosophy. To answer the question of how the universe originated, rather than positing a creator god, classical myth told of the formation of earth and the heavenly bodies from the death and subsequent transformation of a giant creature named Pan Gu. His arms and legs became mountain ranges, his hair vegetation, his eyes the sun and moon, and the blood in his veins rivers and streams. The vermin crawling on his body became the black-haired masses (that is, the Chinese people). In an earlier myth, the death of the faceless emperor Hundun (Chaos) represented the birth of human consciousness (fourth century BCE). What in the mythical worldview was perceived as a transformation of the body into the cosmos was, eventually, in the philosophical mind perceived to be a complex, almost mathematical, correspondence between the human microcosm and the macrocosm of time and space.

One of the early cosmogonies (second century BCE) answers the ontological question of what constituted the cosmos: Out of the nebulous void grew space and time, which generated primordial *qi*. *Qi* (sometimes spelled *ch'i*) is almost impossible to translate in a word or even a phrase. It may help to think of it in the same way Einstein urged his students to think of rocks as "frozen energy." In the swirl of *qi* grew a horizon, above which spread the pure and bright *qi* to form heaven, and below which gathered the heavy and turbid *qi* to form earth. The superposition of heaven and earth produced *yin* and *yang*, and their intermingling produced the myriad things—to heaven belong the sun, moon, and stars, to earth, the waters and soil (*Huainanzi*, 3.1). Heaven (with its revolving sun and moon) is round like the human head (with its ears and eyes), whereas earth, spreading out in four directions, is rectangular (like the squarely planted feet). The four seasons correspond to the four limbs, the twelve months to the twelve joints of the limbs, and wind and rain to the blood and *qi* of the body.

This holistic, organismic view of the cosmos had begun to form at the very latest around 300 BCE, when the following passage was recorded in the *Guanzi*: "Water is the blood *qi* of the earth, flowing and communicating as if in sinews and veins." Previous to this metaphorical use of the term to depict terrestrial water, *qi* was primarily used to explain human physiology. In the fifth or sixth century BCE, the term was used to indicate the "blood and breath," or the pulse, of the human body (*Analects*). It was also used in its modern sense to describe states of emotion, such as *yongqi*, a "spirit of bravery," and *keqi*, "courtesy." Thus, among other things, *qi* was something like the medieval Western concept of humors, the bodily fluids that determined a person's temperament. So the image in *Guanzi* is of living water pulsing underground, emerging as springs, and coursing in rivers.

But *qi* also had other manifestations. One of the earliest uses of the concept of *qi* refers to the six *qi* of heaven—*yin* and *yang*, wind and rain, dark and light—which "descend and produce the five tastes" but "produce the six diseases when they are in excess" (*Zuo Commentary*). We can see in this statement the remnants of a primitive empirical science attempting to seek the causes of diseases in the weather. The passage continues, "an excess of *yin* leads to chills, and of *yang*, to fever; of wind, to diseases of the limbs, and of rain, to diseases of the stomach; of darkness, to delusion, and of light, to diseases of the mind." *Yang* and *yin* at this stage in the evolution of Chinese cosmology are simply two types of *qi*—heat and cold, derived from their literal meanings of sunshine and shade—and have yet to subsume all binary paradigms (such as light and dark, male and female, and so on). Thus far, *qi* is discussed only in its concrete, differentiated aspects and has yet to be abstracted. Eventually, *qi* will be the very foundation of Chinese cosmology, the "universal fluid, active as Yang and passive as Yin, out of which all things condense and into which they dissolve."*

By the time the historical text, the *Guoyu*, or *Discourses of the States*, was completed in the fourth or fifth century BCE, *yin* and *yang* had been elevated to the status of the primary manifestations of *qi*. The following passage, recording the words of the Grand Historian of Zhou, is the earliest known cosmological theory of *qi*: "The *qi* of heaven and earth do not lose their order. If they exceed their order, the people will fall into chaos. If the *yang* is submerged and cannot emerge, and the *yin* is oppressed and cannot rise, there will be earthquakes" (1/10). In another passage from the same text, we see a characterization of *qi* that is more geophysical than cosmological. Here, Prince Jin is trying to dissuade his father, King Ling of Zhou, from damming the rivers to protect the palace from floods:

> I have heard that those who ruled the people in ancient times did not tear down the mountains, nor did they raise the marshes, nor did they obstruct the rivers, nor did they drain the swamps. For mountains are accumulations of earth, and marshes are gathering places for creatures. Rivers are channels for energy [*qi*], and swamps are concentrations of water. When heaven and earth became complete, they had accumulated the high (mountains) and gathered creatures in the low (marshes). They had cut through rivers and valleys, to channel their energy, and dammed and diked stagnant and low-lying water, to concentrate their fertility. For this reason the accumulations (mountains) do not crumble and collapse, and so creatures have a place (marshes) in which to gather. Energy is not sunken and congealed, nor is it scattered and dissipated. Through this the people, when living, have wealth and useful things, and when dead, have places to be buried. (3/3) †

---

*A. C. Graham, *Disputers of the Tao: Philosophical Argument in Ancient China* (La Salle, IL: Open Court, 1989), p. 101.
†Translations from the *Guoyu* are by James A. Hart, in Henry Rosemont, ed. *Explorations in Early Chinese Cosmology* (Chico, CA: Scholars Press, 1984), p. 39.

Here we see that the concept of the accumulation and dispersal of earth and water was the accepted explanation for the appearance of the phenomenal world. The rivers that cut through the accumulated earth channel the *qi* and prevent it from congealing. When swamps are allowed to concentrate the waters, the *qi* is prevented from scattering and dissipating. This view supports principles similar to those of accumulation and dispersal that govern Form School *fengshui*. In addition, when Prince Jin says that the dead will "have places to be buried," he probably refers to a belief in something like burial site *fengshui*, the subject of the *Book of Burial* (see chapter 4 below). His recognition of this fact follows right after his statement that *qi* not be congealed or scattered, which is a requirement for proper burial. Prince Jin continues his persuasion using a historical perspective. He tries to convince his father of the folly of the latter's plan by praising the exploits of Yu the Great, who dredged the rivers, rather than damming them: "He raised the high, lowered the low, dredged the rivers to channel the congealed, and concentrated the (swamp) waters to make abundant the living things. . . . Therefore heaven had no hidden yin, and earth had no scattered yang. There were no waters in which the energy was sunken." In this passage, it is clear that *qi* is separate from water, a departure from the view of the author of *Guanzi*. *Qi* must be "channeled" or guided, presumably to prevent it from congealing, and water follows these courses and thereby avoids stagnation.

This passage is one of the earliest codifications of the theory of conglomeration and dispersal, a concept that was widespread by the early Han dynasty when it had expanded to govern the physiological *qi*. In chapter 22 of the Daoist classic *Zhuangzi* is this passage: "Man's life is the assembling of *qi*. The assembling is called birth, the dispersal is called death." So by the Han dynasty the concept of agglomeration and dispersal of *qi* had both macrocosmic and microcosmic applications.

But the cosmology of *qi* was still not complete. Perhaps the main reason for seeking correspondences between human and natural phenomena is the need to control human civilization by aligning it with natural cycles and patterns. The Chinese thinker whose ideas were most important to the development of a correlative cosmology, the man whose theories may be responsible for the very survival of the philosophy of *qi*, is a shadowy figure named Zou Yan who lived during the first half of the third century BCE. None of his works survives, but he is credited with elaborating on a preexisting system that posited five categories of *qi* rather than two. Most likely originating as gods of the five visible planets (called "moving stars" in Chinese), the five categories were given the seemingly elemental designations water, metal, fire, earth, and wood, and were collectively referred to as *wuxing* (originally mistranslated as "five elements" but now called the "five phases" or "movements"). Rather than being constituent material elements of the world, these categories refer instead to phases that are inherently connected. At least a century before Zou Yan, these processes had already been linked to two orders of transmutation called the mutual production (or generation) and mutual conquest orders, reproduced in table 1. Zou Yan's unique contribution to the history of Chinese cosmology was to correlate what he called the "five powers" with the cyclical patterns of human history so that the rise and fall of dynasties could be predicted. For this reason, he was the favorite of every hegemonic power seeking to seize the mandate of heaven from the declining Zhou dynasty. Under the patronage of some of the most powerful kings of the Warring States (403–221 BCE), Zou was able to refine his theories and disseminate them widely.

At this time in Chinese history, one of the oldest correlations, that between the cycle of the four seasons and the square of the four cardinal directions, was matched with the sequence of the five phases. The fire phase was the natural match for summer and south, while the wood phase, the process of vegetal growth, matched east and spring. Fire and water were long represented in literature as a dyadic pair, so water was matched with north and winter. Soil was the obvious choice

TABLE 1. PRODUCTION AND CONQUEST ORDERS OF THE FIVE PHASES

Mutual Production Order	Mutual Conquest Order
Earth harbors metal (ores)	Earth dams water
Metal condenses water (on bronze mirrors)	Water quenches fire
Water nourishes wood (plants)	Fire melts metal
Wood feeds fire	Metal cuts wood
Fire builds earth (as ashes)	Wood saps earth

for the center of the earth, since all the other phases either originated in soil (the ores of metal, and growing wood) or terminated there (the ash of fire, and soaking water). That left the metal phase to be matched with autumn and west. With these correlations established, beginning in the center with soil and following the natural order of the seasons, the whole sequence was interpreted as the order in which the phases generate each other throughout the year. See figure 1 for a spatial representation of this series (in traditional Chinese cartography, south, rather than north, is placed at the top of the map).

Every conceivable structural relation reducible to a factor of five was now correlated with the five phases. Red is the natural color of fire, yellow is the color of the soil that gave the Yellow River its name, growing vegetation is green, deep bodies of water are black, and metal salts are white. Fire rises, and feathered creatures ascend. Water sinks, and shelled creatures dive. Vegetation sheds its leaves and lies dormant, and scaly creatures shed their skin and hibernate. In similar fashion, the sense organs and visceral organs of the human body, agricultural products, land animals, and so on, are all correlated with the five phases. With these associations established, the generation and conquest orders of the phases are then keys to properly affecting the natural process of particular organisms and organs. For example, wood governs the liver, and water nourishes wood. Legumes belong to the element water, so a diet rich in soybeans can be beneficial to

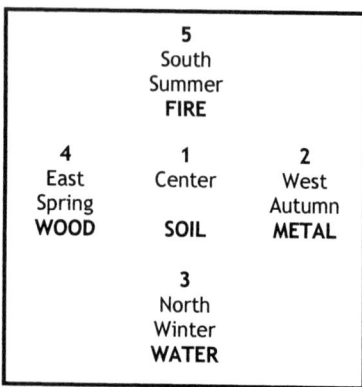

Fig. 1. Production order of the Five Phases

Background: Chinese Correlative Cosmology   13

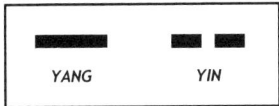

Fig. 2. The two monograms

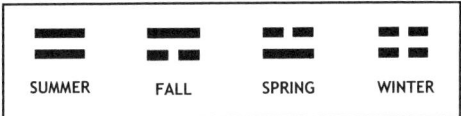

Fig. 3. The four digrams

the liver. Most importantly for the purposes of this book: *knowledge of the current phase of any aspect of a person's life makes it possible to project its future characteristic.* This is the foundation of much of Chinese divination.*

At the same time that Zou Yan was perfecting his five-term system, philosophers were developing an eight-term system based on the graphic images of the *Zhou Changes*. The symbolic structure of that book is also a microcosm of the phenomenal world but is so abstract as to be almost unrecognizable. Yet its organization and symbols are some of the most pervasive in Chinese philosophy. No description of Chinese cosmology would be complete without a thorough understanding of the *bagua,* or "eight trigrams," of the *Zhou Changes*. The most fundamental image of this system is the "monogram," composed of either a solid *yang* line, representing hardness and movement, or the broken *yin* line, representing softness and rest (see fig. 2). These two lines combine to form the "digram," representing the four seasons (see fig. 3). Two *yang* lines characterize summer, whereas two *yin* lines represent winter. The potential progress of lines within a figure is organically upward, so a *yang* line encroaching upon a *yin* line is spring, and a *yin* line encroaching upon a *yang* line is autumn.

---

*For example, see the discussion of the Eight-House system of *fengshui* at the end of chapter 4. See also the section on *rishu* (daybooks) at the beginning of chapter 7.

Qian	Dui	Li	Zhen	Xun	Kan	Gen	Kun
☰	☱	☲	☳	☴	☵	☶	☷
HEAVEN	LAKE	FIRE	THUNDER	WOOD	WATER	MOUNTAIN	EARTH
1	2	3	4	5	6	7	8

Fig. 4. The eight trigrams

PUSHING
UPWARD
46

Fig. 5. A hexagram

A "trigram" is composed of a combination of three *yang* and/or *yin* lines for a total of eight separate figures, each exhibiting unique characteristics (see fig. 4). Three *yang* lines denote heaven; three *yin* lines denote earth. A *yang* line sandwiched between two *yin* lines denotes water; the opposite denotes fire. Two *yang* lines topped with a *yin* line form lake; two *yin* lines topped with a *yang* line form mountain. One *yang* line below two *yin* lines forms thunder; the opposite forms wood or wind. Finally, two trigrams combine to form a "hexagram" (see fig. 5). For example, the trigram for "earth" over the trigram for "wood" forms hexagram 46, "Pushing Upward" (because plants push up through soil). Eight trigrams combine for a total of sixty-four hexagrams, each of which is an archetype of the phenomenal world. The totality of sixty-four hexagrams, each of which contains discrete lines of significance, and the countless permutations of meaning suggested by the complex interaction between hexagram, trigram, and line, capture the multivalent complexity of the natural world and human civilization (see pp. 39–41).

By the Han dynasty, when cosmological speculations were at their height, the text and figures of the *Zhou Changes* were subjected to intense scrutiny. As a result, the trigrams became a correlative goldmine, and the paradigm of eight joined that of two and five to become

Background: Chinese Correlative Cosmology 15

one of the most enduring of the many cosmological structures. In particular, two configurations of those eight trigrams formed the theoretical foundation of many forms of Chinese fortune-telling. They are known as the *xiantian* (pre-heaven) and *houtian* (post-heaven) orders and are illustrated in figures 6 and 7, accompanied by the English translations of the trigram attributes.

When configured in a square with three cells to a side, the postheaven sequence of eight trigrams could then be correlated with the square earth and its eight directions (four cardinal directions and the

DUI Lake	QIAN Heaven	XUN Wood
LI Fire		KAN Water
ZHEN Thunder	KUN Earth	GEN Mountain

Fig. 6. Pre-heaven trigrams

XUN Wood	LI Fire	KUN Earth
ZHEN Thunder		DUI Lake
GEN Mountain	KAN Water	QIAN Heaven

Fig. 7. Post-heaven trigrams

XUN Wood SE	LI Fire South	KUN Earth SW
ZHEN Thunder East	Center	DUI Lake West
GEN Mountain NE	KAN Water North	QIAN Heaven NW

Fig. 8. The Palace of Nine Halls

four corners), which is known as the *jiugong*, or "palace of nine halls" (see fig. 8). A trigram and one of the eight directions represent each of eight of the nine halls. The direction identifies its location in space, and the trigram characterizes the *qi* of that location. The ninth hall is the courtyard of the palace.

Other correlations were also being made. For example, in the "Trigram Explanation" commentary to the *Zhou Changes*, the trigrams of the post-heaven sequence were given seasonal associations in addition to agricultural connotations, which added a temporal component to the spatial layout (thunder in the east represented spring planting; fire in the south represented summer growth; lake in the west represented autumn harvest; and water in the north represented winter storage). In addition, when the five-phase qualities were grafted onto the square, the post-heaven sequence corresponded to the production order of the five phases (see fig. 16 in chap. 4). In such fashion, fire and water joined their trigrammatic counterparts in the south and north. The soil phase joined its counterpart earth in the southwest, in addition to mountain in the northeast. The wood phase joined its trigram counterpart in the southeast in addition to the trigram thunder in the east. And the metal phase was attached to the trigrams lake and heaven in the west and northwest.

At least as early as the Han dynasty (206 BCE–220 CE), the post-heaven configuration of trigrams was also correlated with a sequence of numbers known as *luoshu*, or the Luo (River) Writing (see fig. 9). The Luo Writing is first mentioned in the Confucian *Analects,* and the Daoist philosopher Zhuangzi first mentioned the "nine numbers" of the Luo. The "Appended Words" commentary of the *Zhou Changes* first connected the Luo Writing with another configuration known as *hetu,* or (Yellow) River Chart (see fig. 10). The three-by-three-square grid of the Luo Writing is also called the "magic square" because all rows, columns, and diagonals add up to fifteen. This numerical configuration is the basis of Chinese Compass School *fengshui* and is perhaps the most complex aspect of Chinese cosmology. Han

Wood 4	Fire 9	Earth 2
Thunder 3	5	Lake 7
Mountain 8	Water 1	Heaven 6

Fig. 9. The Luo Writing numbers and post-heaven trigrams

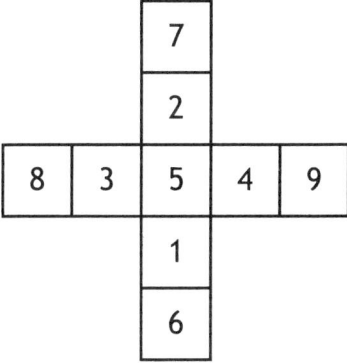

Fig. 10. The River Chart numbers

dynasty tombs excavated in the last decades of the twentieth century contained examples of astronomical and astrological instruments inscribed with the numbers of the magic square in addition to the post-heaven sequence of trigrams. Such instruments were called *shi*, or models of the cosmos, and were constructed of a heaven disc that rotated atop a square earth plate. These divination boards (dubbed "cosmographs") were correlative masterpieces (see pp. 92–95 for a discussion of one such divination board).

Another set of correlations also had temporal connotations but only in the sense that a sequence of figures could be chosen to represent the incremental passage of time. This chronological classification system was formed of two separate series, one of ten terms with a heavenly attribution—the *tiangan* (heaven stems), originally designating days of the week, and one of twelve terms with an earthly provenance—the *dizhi* (earth branches), denoting months of the year. When combined they formed a sixty-term (sexagesimal, or sexidecimal) cycle that linked heaven and earth in one organic whole.* Appropriately, both sets of terms inscribe the circumference of the cosmograph (see fig. 20). Tables 2 and 3 outline the two components of this numbering system, giving names and various correlates.

As we have seen, for the Chinese, correlation between categories depended primarily on their fundamental numerical values. The opening chapter of the major text of Daoism, the *Laozi,* says: "The *dao* gave birth to the one, the one gave birth to the two, the two gave birth to the three, and the three gave birth to the ten-thousand things." This is nothing more than a numerological cosmogony, whose basic numerical categories I have attempted to enumerate while also explaining how they interacted. Out of the *dao* was born *qi*, the monad, the most fundamental stuff of the cosmos. From the unity of *qi* split categories of two, all correlated with *yin* and *yang*. The coupling of *yin* and *yang* gave birth to a third entity, and the three branched into

---

* Creating the sexagesimal cycle is like placing six ten-inch *stem* rulers (a total of sixty inches) end-to-end above five twelve-inch *branch* rulers, also end-to-end. Each stem inch (numbered 1–10) then has a corresponding branch inch (labeled A–L), creating sixty unique two-term combinations called "pillars." The sexagesimal cycle begins with *jiazi* (1A) and ends with *guihai* (10L).

Background: Chinese Correlative Cosmology

TABLE 2. THE HEAVEN STEMS

Sequence	Stem Name	Polarity	Phase
1	Jia	*Yang*	Wood
2	Yi	*Yin*	Wood
3	Bing	*Yang*	Fire
4	Ding	*Yin*	Fire
5	Wu	*Yang*	Earth
6	Ji	*Yin*	Earth
7	Geng	*Yang*	Metal
8	Xin	*Yin*	Metal
9	Ren	*Yang*	Water
10	Gui	*Yin*	Water

TABLE 3. THE EARTH BRANCHES

Sequence	Branch Name	Symbolic Animal	Polarity	Phase	Month	Double-Hour
A	Zi	Rat	*Yang*	Water	1st	11–1 a.m.
B	Chou	Ox	*Yin*	Earth	2nd	1–3
C	Yin	Tiger	*Yang*	Wood	3rd	3–5
D	Mao	Rabbit	*Yin*	Wood	4th	5–7
E	Chen	Dragon	*Yang*	Earth	5th	7–9
F	Si	Snake	*Yin*	Fire	6th	9–11
G	Wu	Horse	*Yang*	Fire	7th	11–1 p.m.
H	Wei	Sheep	*Yin*	Earth	8th	1–3
I	Shen	Monkey	*Yang*	Metal	9th	3–5
J	You	Rooster	*Yin*	Metal	10th	5–7
K	Xu	Dog	*Yang*	Earth	11th	7–9
L	Hai	Pig	*Yin*	Water	12th	9–11

four, five, eight, twelve, twenty-eight, sixty, sixty-four, and so on, all the way to *wanwu*, the Chinese word for "myriad things," that is, everything in the phenomenal world.

Aspects of the correlative scheme enumerated above became patterns for the proto-sciences of astrology, fate-calculation, the healing arts, alchemy, and *fengshui*. They were proto-sciences in their earliest stages because they were loosely based on empirical observation—the first prerequisite for the scientific method. However, the second characteristic of scientific questioning is to seek an explanation for an occurrence, which normally takes the form of a cause-and-effect relationship verifiable by experimentation. Once the logic of causality overtook correlative thinking, some proto-sciences would develop into the sciences of astronomy and medicine. The remainder would join the realm of the pseudosciences, those systems of thought whose correlative schemes, although superficially logical, nevertheless cannot be scientifically validated. This book is concerned only with the pseudoscientific systems. In particular, it is the schematizing logic of the diviners that I will seek to unravel in the course of my discussions. With this basic understanding of Chinese cosmology, I will now proceed with chapter 2 of the analysis, a chronological account of the early development of divination by number and image.

CHAPTER 2

The Origin and Evolution of Chinese Divination

The two earliest forms of divination for which there is historical evidence used either the reading of divinatory cracks in scorched turtle shells or the numinous counting of stalks of the milfoil plant (also called yarrow). However, recent discoveries indicate that counting may have played an important role in divination thousands of years earlier. At this early stage of divination, turtles appear to have been used for counting rather than for the production of divinatory images. The counting of milfoil stalks that appeared much later in the tradition was thus preceded by another form of divination that also recognized the mystical quality of numbers.

The further back we must go to find the origin of cultural artifacts, the more likely the origins will remain shrouded in mystery. That is certainly the case with Chinese divination, whose earliest trace can be glimpsed in the burial goods of Neolithic tombs. In this chapter we will look closely at several tombs that hold evidence of turtle divination, indicating that the Chinese of nine thousand years ago may have worshipped a turtle spirit.

Neolithic Divination

The earliest evidence of divination in China was discovered in a site dating to the seventh millennium BCE, a prehistoric village of some fifty houses and eleven pottery kilns that also contained 439 graves. Its culture was dubbed "Jiahu" by archaeologists, after the modern town at the site of the excavation. In about 5 percent of the graves were discovered turtle shells placed by the head, feet, or thigh of the deceased. Some of the shells were incised with symbols that archaeologists speculate may be early precursors of writing in ancient China.

In one man's grave, the skull was replaced by eight sets of turtle shells and a fork-shaped bone artifact. In the lower center of one plastron (breastplate) in the group of eight was carved a symbol resembling the word for "eye" as seen in later Shang dynasty inscriptions. A second grave that also contained eight sets of turtle shells produced a plastron with an inscribed symbol resembling the word for the number "eight" in Shang script. In the same grave, a broken carapace (shell) is incised with a sign that appears to be a person holding a fork-shaped object. Several sets of turtle shells had holes bored along the edges so that carapace and plastron could be tied together with cord to form "boxes." All such boxes contained pebbles of varying numbers but of similar size and of either dark or light colors. Finally, more than thirty bone flutes were discovered, all manufactured from the wing bone of the red-crowned crane. These are the earliest musical instruments known. Many scholars believe that these artifacts clearly point to the practice of divination. At the very least, the turtle boxes filled with pebbles could have functioned as musical rattles that, along with the flutes, may have been used in shamanistic rituals. But the boxes may also have functioned as very primitive numerical calculators in the early practice of numerology, or the casting of auspicious numbers.

Similar turtle shell boxes were buried with the deceased in another site dated five thousand years later. One turtle found sacrificed atop the left abdomen of the tomb occupant was pierced with four holes in both carapace and plastron in a square configuration. The top and bottom were incised with X-shaped cord marks, clearly indicating how the box was fastened together. In a 3600 BCE site near Liangjiatan in Anhui Province, a carved jade turtle was discovered that is reminiscent of the earlier turtles in its configuration of bored holes and grooves for cords. However, instead of multicolored stones, a rectangular jade plate with an intricate carving was inserted between the carapace and plastron of the jade turtle (see fig. 11).

In the center of the plate is a small square surrounded by eight wedges inscribed in a circle; outside this circle is another circle, which is divided into eight pie-shaped segments, inside each of which is an arrow-shaped figure further divided into eight sections. Outside this circle are four more eight-sectioned arrows, pointing toward the

The Origin and Evolution of Chinese Divination

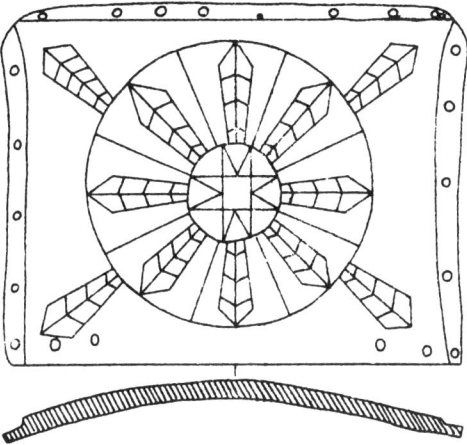

Fig. 11. Line drawing of the jade plate (after Wenwu *1989, no. 4, p. 15)*

four corners of the rectangular plate. The full significance of the symbol will probably remain a mystery, but we can at least surmise that it is related to the cosmological worldview of the ancients. Perhaps the four external arrows depict the four corners of the square earth, which extend beyond the circular heaven of eight segments (compare this to the myth fragment below, which states that "the sky did not cover everywhere"). The internal arrows might point to each of the eight directions or the origin of the eight winds. In the center of the dome of heaven is a circular ninth section, enclosing an eight-pointed figure, possibly a representation of the North Star or even the sun; another jade artifact discovered at the same site is carved in the shape of a bird with an eight-pointed sun symbol carved in its belly. Clearly, the number eight is of primary importance to this form of early divination.

As to the relationship between the multicolored pebbles of the Jiahu turtle boxes and the cosmic diagram of the Liangjiatan jade turtle, we can only speculate. The pebbles are reminiscent of chess pieces and counters in the Han dynasty divinatory game called *liubo*, or Six Wands, which was played with six bamboo counting sticks and twelve ivory chessmen. The jade plate reminds us of both the *liubo* board and the *liuren* cosmograph, divinatory instruments that will be discussed in some detail in chapter 5. Some scholars even speculate that the jade plate is the origin of the myth of the Luo Writing figure, which supposedly appeared on the back of a turtle emerging from the Luo River. Other scholars have suggested that the pebbles enabled diviners to communicate with the turtle spirit in at least two ways. When the shaken turtle was opened, the configuration of the pebbles was observed, with the pattern of odd numbers and even numbers of pebbles determining auspicious or inauspicious readings. A second possibility concerns the shade of the pebbles, which were either dark or light. The distinction would enable the diviner to visualize an image in addition to a number in the divination ritual. For example, light stones could represent the sun or heaven, and perhaps fire, whereas dark stones could represent the moon or earth, and perhaps water. Although many centuries would pass before the Chinese abstracted the concepts of *yin* and *yang* out of the natural binary categories, it is fascinating to see that the prehistoric shamans were perhaps already beginning to reason thusly. If this speculation is plausible, the Jiahu pebbles are the likely origin of divination by image. That the function of numbers may have been related to differences in color in the divination ritual suggests that the ancient diviners had already begun to think comprehensively, for the distinction between number and image would remain the defining quality of Chinese divination.

It is not possible to know anything more about the turtle spirit as conceived in the Neolithic period than what these burial goods can tell us by their shape and perceived function. However, from numerous turtle references that survive in fragments of Chinese myth, we can make some educated guesses regarding the status of the turtle in late Neolithic China. By the dawn of Chinese history, the diminutive animal had become a microcosm of the entire world—that is to say, the vault of the heavens is a gigantic turtle shell suspended above the earth atop four mountain-like turtle legs standing at the corners of the world. Two myths evidencing the antiquity of this worldview are recorded in the second-century BCE *Huainanzi*:

> Previously, when Gong Gong fought with Zhuan Xu to become Lord [*Di*], in his rage, he butted the Mountain which cannot be circumnavigated (*Buzhou*). The sky's pillar was broken and the tie

with the earth severed. The sky inclined to the northwest, and so the heavenly bodies move in that direction. The earth was not full in the southeast, and so the water and dust go there. (3.1)

In a time long ago, the four poles were decayed and the nine states rent asunder. The sky did not cover everywhere and the earth was not filled in all around. Fire raged and flamed without dying out; water swelled and rose without dying down. Fierce beasts ate the vigorous and vultures snatched the old and weak. Then, Nü Wa smelted stones of five colors and patched up the azure sky and cut off the legs of a sea-turtle to stand up the four poles. (6.6)*

Nü Wa was the half-human, half-dragon goddess who formed humans out of yellow clay.

Other myths are also clues to the existence of prehistoric turtle gods. Gun, son of Zhuan Xu in the account above, attempted to quell the floods that were consequent upon the destruction of Mount Buzhou, but he failed and lay dying in the abysmal realm of the Quill Depths. Before he died, however, he gave birth to a son named Yu, then he transformed himself into a three-legged turtle and plunged into the abyss. The son subsequently quelled the floods and founded the Xia dynasty when he placed his own son, Prince Qi, on the throne. He was known thereafter as Yu the Great.

Scapulimancy and Plastromancy

Bone cracking for the purpose of divination had been prevalent in cultural areas of Neolithic China at least since the third millennium BCE. Known as pyro-osteomancy, after its basic methodology, bone divination in China consisted of heating an animal bone to crack it and then observing the crack to determine the fortune. The most commonly used bones were bovine shoulder blades, which provided large, flat working surfaces, but the scapula of deer, sheep, horses, and swine were also used. Scholars call this form of divination scapulimancy. The technique used by the earliest Sinitic cultures was prob-

---

*These myth fragments are translated by Sarah Allan in *The Shape of the Turtle: Myth, Art, and Cosmos in Early China* (Albany: State University of New York Press, 1991), pp. 104–105.

ably similar to that still used by Mongolians who divine by sheep scapula. The divination ceremony begins with the ritual address, when the shaman explains the situation under inquiry. Then the bone is spat upon and placed in the fire. When cracks appear, depending on whether they are straight and long, or short and crooked, the fortune is determined to be auspicious or inauspicious. By the late Shang dynasty (c. 1200 BCE), it was the plastron or undershell of the turtle that was the preferred medium of divination. Scholars therefore call this technique plastromancy.

Before the actual divination, the shoulder blade of the ox or the shell of the turtle was specially prepared. The spine and socket of the shoulder blade were sawn off so that the bone was flat on both sides (see fig. 12). The carapace of the turtle was sawn apart from the plastron. All surfaces were scraped and planed to present the smoothest face possible. Then, several rows of paired indentations were carved on the back, each pair consisting of a shallow, circular, bored pit and, tangent to this, a vertical, oblong, deeply chiseled groove. When a red-hot brand was applied to the center of the chiseled pit, two cracks would appear on the opposite side of the bone or shell — a vertical crack corresponding to the oblong groove and, perpendicular to this, a horizontal crack extending into the circular hollow. The crack would thus look something like the Chinese character *bu*, pronounced *puk* in archaic Chinese, an onomatopoeic representation of the noise of a bone cracking. At least in the formative stages of Chinese pyro-osteomancy, the cracks answered the questions of kings, as put to the spirits by diviners. It was the gods or spirits who were speaking, and the kings and their diviners interpreted the divine language of the pyromantic cracks in bone or shell. I excerpt here a fanciful description of how such a ritual might have proceeded, as conceived by David Keightley, the scholar who has written most informatively on the subject.

An Ancient Crack-making Ceremony

Filtering through the portal of the ancestral temple, the sunlight wakens the eyes of the monster mask, bulging with life on the garish bronze tripod. At the center of the temple stands the king, at the center of the four quarters, the center of the Shang world. Ripening millet glimpsed through the doorway shows his harvest rituals have

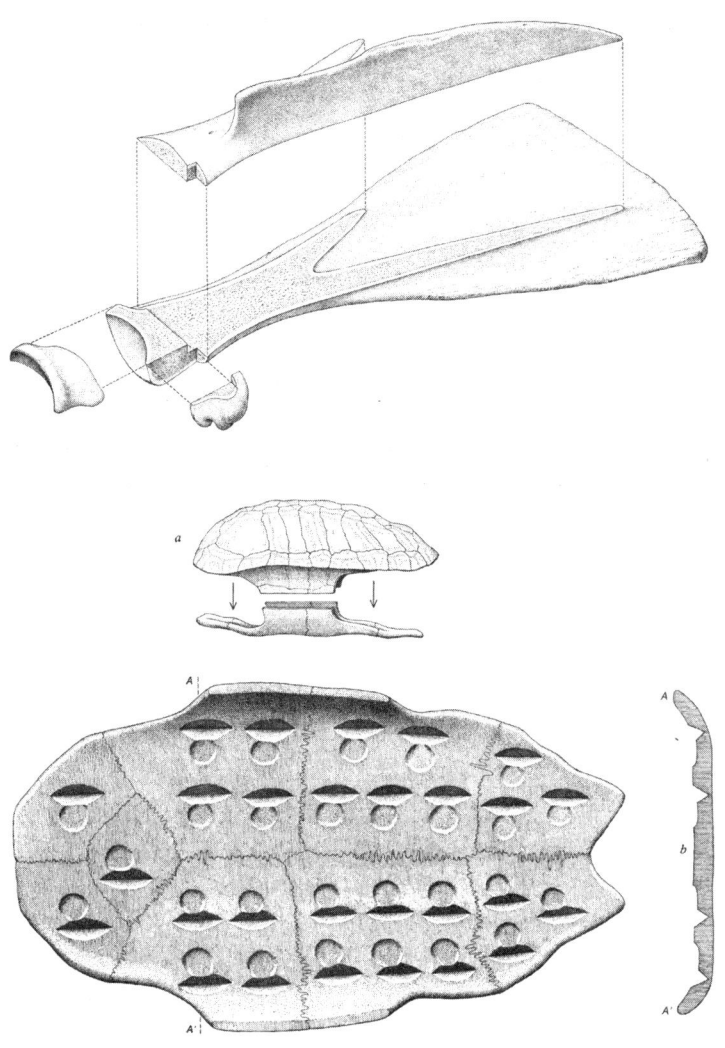

Fig. 12. Scapula and plastron preparation (after Scientific American *April 1979, p. 138)*

found favor. Bronze cauldrons with their cooked meat offerings invite the presence of his ancestors, their bodies buried deep and safely across the river, but their spirits, some benevolent, some not, still reigning over the royal house and the king's person. One is angry, for the king's jaw ached all the night, is aching now, on the eve of his departure to follow Zhi Guo on campaign against the Bafang.

Five turtle shells lie on the rammed-earth altar. The plastrons have been polished like jade, but are scarred on their inner side with rows of oval hollows, some already blackened by fire. Into one of the unburned hollows, on the right side of the shell, the diviner Que is thrusting a brand of flaming thorn. As he does so, he cries aloud, "The sick tooth is not due to Father Jia!" Fanned by an assistant to keep the glowing tip intensely hot, the stick flames against the surface of the shell. Smoke rises. The seconds slowly pass. The stench of scorched bone mingles with the aroma of millet wine scattered in libation. And then, with a sharp, clear, *puk*-like sound, the turtle, most silent of creatures, speaks. A *bu*-shaped crack has formed in the hollow where the plastron was scorched. Once again the brand is thrust, now into a matching hollow on the left side of the shell: "It is due to Father Jia!" More time passes . . . another crack forms in response. Moving to the next plastron, Que repeats the charges: "It is not due to Father Jia!" *Puk*! "It is due to Father Jia!" He rams the brand into the hollows and cracks the second turtle shell, then the third, the fourth, and the fifth.

The diviners consult. The congregation of kinsmen strains to catch their words, for the curse of a dead father may, in the king's eyes, be the work of a living son. Que rubs wood ash from the fire into the new set of cracks and scrutinizes them once more. But the shell has given no indication. The charge must be divined again. Two more cracks are made in each of the five plastrons . . . and there is again no sign.

Another brand is plucked from the fire and the new charge cried: "The sick tooth is not due to Father Geng! . . . It is due to Father Geng." Father Geng—the king's senior uncle. This time the indications are clear. His sons, the king's older cousins, turn away in dismay at the diviner's reading of the cracks. The spirit, their father, has been blamed. But still the work of spiritual identification continues. "It is not due to Father Xin! . . . It is due to Father Xin!" Que moves methodically down the row of five plastrons, reciting the negative and positive charges and cracking each shell twice in this way. No judgment can be made. Once again, as for Father Jia, ten more cracks are burned. "Auspicious!" Que points to two cracks on the second and fourth shells. Father Xin is without blame, his descendants relieved. . . .

    Now the king speaks. Assistants drag two victims into the temple. There is the barking and bleating of animals in panic, then silence. Blood stains the earth floor. The king dismembers the victims as Que proposes a new charge: "I sacrifice a dog to Father Geng, and butcher a sheep." The brand flames . . . *puk* . . . *puk* . . . *puk* . . . the plastrons crack in slow and stately sequence. Has the sacrifice mollified the dead uncle? Will the pain in the sick tooth depart? The king, his hands still sticky with blood, scans the cracks.

After the crack-making ceremony, the charges, prognostications, date, and diviner's name were written on the oracle bones with brush and ink. Then they were carried to the archive behind the temple. When the ten-day week was over and the result of the prognostication was known, the archivist carved the information and sometimes the result of the prognostication into the bones. The entire record would look something like the information in table 4, which became the standard formula for the oracle bone text.

TABLE 4. ANALYSIS OF A SHANG ORACLE BONE INSCRIPTION

Type of inscription	Positive left side of plastron	Negative right side
Preface	Crack-making on day 6D (16th), Que divined:	Crack-making on day 6D (16th), Que divined:
Charge	"It will rain."	"It will not perhaps rain."
Prognostication	The king, reading the cracks said: "It will rain; it will be a 9-stem day."	
Verification	On day 9G (19th) it did rain.	

In this text a diviner named Que performs the crack-making ceremony with the charge, "It will (or will not) rain." Then the king reads the resulting cracks and utters the prognostication, "It will rain; it will be a 9-stem day." Note in this account that it is the king who conducts the prognostication, not the professional diviner. Since the king was a direct descendant of the spirits being consulted, it is natural to assume that the ancestral spirit was communicating to him or speaking through him. Using a pair of antithetical questions, as appears in table 4, was also standard practice (as we noted in the fictional account of the ritual above); it indicates that the oracle gives a yes or no answer. Scapulimancy and plastromancy continued in the Western Han dynasty (206 BCE–25 CE), although for the most part their use in the court was superseded by milfoil divination.

The process by which the king's prognostication proceeded from the diviner's charge is unclear from the bone record but can be clarified by looking at a Zhou dynasty bone-cracking ceremony taken from the annals of Duke Xiang, tenth year (563 BCE), in the *Zuo Commentary* to the Confucian *Spring and Autumn Annals*. While the ruler of Wei was away on a military campaign, his land was attacked. Sun Wenzi, a nobleman of Wei, was considering whether or not to launch a counterattack.

> Sun Wenzi cracked a turtle shell regarding pursuit, and then presented the crack to the ruler's mother Ding Jiang. Lady Jiang asked for the verse. He said:
> A crack like a mountain overhanging.
> There was a chief who led a raid.
> Instead, 'twas he who lost his braves.

This three-line oracular verse rhymed in the original Chinese, which suggests that Sun Wenzi chose it from an oral repertoire or retrieved it from some kind of diviner's manual. By his choice of words, the diviner implies that the mountain-shaped crack is oppressive, or symbolic of usurpation. The attached omen—about a raider who loses his warriors—is therefore directed at Huang'er, the usurper. Sun Wenzi then requested counsel from Lady Jiang to determine the outcome of his impending counterattack. She said, "The raider's loss of braves is what you will gain from opposing the bandits." In this bone-cracking ceremony, Lady Jiang takes the place of the king in the Shang dynasty ritual. In the absence of the Wei king, the king's mother was the most appropriate person to interpret the language of the ancestors. Had the queen mother added at the end of her counsel a prognostication such as "An attack will bring good fortune," the entire episode would be identical to the form of a standard hexagram text from the *Zhou Changes*. The *Zuo Commentary* passage concludes with the following verification: "The great officers laid the plans, the people of Wei pursued them, and Sun Kuai captured Huang'er of Zheng at Hound Hill." Although the Shang and Zhou crack-making rituals are separated by several centuries, they maintain the same basic format of preface, charge, prognostication, and verification. As we will see, this format was very similar to the template for the texts of milfoil divination.

Milfoil Divination

Because of the paucity of records, no one is quite sure how divination evolved from the Shang dynasty until the formative phase of milfoil divination in the Spring and Autumn period (722–484 BCE). Fortunately, there are tantalizing passages from later texts that purport to describe much earlier traditions. We begin with this important record of pre-Qin divination procedures from the "Spring Offices" chapter of the Warring States–era text, the *Rites of Zhou*: "The stalk-caster takes charge of the three *Changes* and designates the names of the nine milfoil rites. The first *Change* is called *Linked Mountains*, the second is called *Guicang*, the third is called the *Zhou Changes*." The *Linked Mountains* is reputed to be a divination manual of the Xia dynasty (c. 2070–c. 1600 BCE), the *Guicang* is a Shang dynasty (c. 1600–1046 BCE) divination manual, and the *Zhou Changes* is the Zhou dynasty (1046–256 BCE) divination manual that became a literary classic. Only incomplete portions of the first and second manuals have survived, but there is sufficient information to ascertain differences in the three traditions and therefore draw important conclusions that will influence our perspective on the development of Chinese divination.

While these three manuals may have originated in different periods, they did not supersede each other as the dynasties that spawned them collapsed. Clear examples of various milfoil divination procedures being used simultaneously can be deduced from records in Zhou-era texts. For example, in the *Discourses on the States,* the section on the State of Jin includes an interesting story based on opposing divination methodologies. This passage will appear confusing because I have yet to discuss in any detail such concepts as trigrams and hexagram lines. However, what is important to the current analysis is the differences of opinion that occur when different manuals of divination are used:

> Chong'er, the son of the Duke of Jin, personally cast the milfoil, saying "Who will ascend to the rule of Jin?" He received the lower trigram of Zhun ☳ and the upper trigram of Yu ☳ , both eights. His diviner consulted the manuals, and both of them indicated, "Inauspicious. Obstructed and impenetrable, the lines do not apply." However, Chong'er's loyal follower, Sikong Jizi, said, "On the contrary, it is auspicious. In the *Zhou Changes* both hexagrams say, 'Favorable for appointing to a lordship.' If you, my lord, do not gain the rule of Jin in order to support the royal house, how can anyone be appointed to a lordship? We gave the charge, 'Who will ascend to the rule of Jin?' The milfoil tells us, 'Favorable for appointing to a lordship,' which must mean gaining the reins of state. No fortune could be greater!"

According to this story, the diviner's judgment was overruled. Because the *Zhou Changes* was used to refute the opinion of the diviner, the diviner must have been using something other than the *Zhou Changes*. It is unclear what tradition of milfoil divination is reflected here; however, the lower trigram of Zhun and the upper trigram of Yu are the same trigram — *zhen* (thunder). Its use as the focus of the unorthodox reading probably means that trigrams, rather than individual hexagram lines, were the basis of auspice determination in this form of divination. This distinction will become important later in the chapter because it is likely that the diviner was using the *Linked Mountains* or *Guicang* for his reading. We will now take a closer look at those texts.

There exists a redacted version of the *Linked Mountains* compiled by Ma Guohan in the Qing dynasty. Ma's *Linked Mountains Changes* collects some fifteen fragments from records as old as the *Zuo Commentary*. Of the fifteen fragments, fully a third of them portray demigods and culture heroes connected to the founding of the Xia dynasty. For example, fragment 7 reads, "Chief Gun of Youchong concealed himself in the wilds of Quill Mountain." And fragment 9 reads, "Yu took the child of Tu Mountain as his bride. Her name was Distant Girl; she gave birth to Qi." Ma Guohan also assembled remarks on the *Linked Mountains* gleaned from texts going back to the Zhou dynasty. For example, he quotes Huangfu Mi (215–282 CE), who gave this explanation for the meaning of the book's name: "The pure hexagram Gen begins the *Linked Mountains*. The trigram *gen* means mountain; thus one mountain atop another is 'linked mountains,' the name of the book."

Fragment 12 in the *Linked Mountains* redaction is particularly enlightening. This excerpt appears verbatim in the "Trigram Explanation" commentary of the *Zhou Changes* and is the basis for the configuration of trigrams known as the post-heaven sequence. The following is a literal translation of the excerpt: "The emperor [*di*] emerges in *zhen*, brings order in *xun*, is made manifest in *li*, receives service in *kun*, rejoices in *dui*, battles in *qian*, toils in *kan*, and is complete in *gen*." It would be difficult to derive any narrative meaning from these words because no one is sure what the trigram names meant in that era. To most readers of the "Trigram Explanation" commentary, the content of the passage was incidental to the order of the trigrams as they appeared in the narrative.

Immediately following the passage in the "Trigram Explanation" is an interpretative annotation, which itself attests to the antiquity of the original passage. It also suggests that the meaning was not self-evident and that the compilers of the commentary themselves had already forgotten the reasoning behind the passage. This annotation added the concepts of direction and seasons to the picture, which could then be visualized in this fashion: When arranged in a circle with *zhen* (thunder) in the east—the direction of spring, and *li* (fire) in the south—the direction of summer, and so on, the sequence now combined the dimension of time to the space of heaven and earth. It also replaced "emperor" with *wanwu*, the "myriad things." From this perspective, the passage is an ontological narration of the evolution of the phenomenal world ("the world was born in spring thunder"). But a prehistoric culture was surely not capable of such proto-scientific thought. If we are to believe that this passage originated in the Xia dynasty (2070–1600 BCE), it must somehow realistically reflect the beliefs of a preliterate society.

As I have depicted the origin of divination in China, the Neolithic Chinese believed in a turtle spirit. Furthermore, the Shang nobles spoke to ancestral spirits and other gods in the process of their divination rites. If the passage in question originates in the period between Neolithic China and the Shang dynasty, it is likely that the passage is religious in meaning. Since the learned scholars who authored the commentaries sought to find cosmological import in the *Zhou Changes* symbols, they may have overlooked or ignored any religious significance. The first character in the passage, *di*, eventually would be used in the titles of earthly sovereigns (as with Qin Shihuang*di*, the First Emperor of Qin). But assuming the antiquity of this passage, here it probably refers to a deity or at least a mythical demigod.* The deity worshipped by the Chinese at least since the middle of the Shang dynasty was the "*di* above," or High God, probably an abstracted "first ancestor." If the heavenly *di* is the subject of this passage, then its tone changes completely. Now it is God who emerges in thunder—quite an ominous image. And if one understands *zhen* not as thunder but as an earthquake, another meaning of the term, then the passage becomes even more ominous. Unfortunately, it is not possible to accurately interpret the remainder of the passage, because it is a two- or three-thousand-year-old transmitted written text that ostensibly was itself the record of an oral text. It is sufficient only to point out that the "God emerges" passage from the "Trigram Explanation" commentary is possibly some kind of religious rite that was originally recorded in the Xia dynasty *Linked Mountains*. Therefore,

---

*Previous to the use of *di* by Qin Shihuangdi, the term referred either to Shang Di (the High God) or to mythical and legendary rulers. The latter are collectively referred to as *sanhuang wudi*, the "three sovereigns and five emperors," variously identified as Fuxi, Nü Wa, and Shen Nong (the Divine Farmer), plus Huang Di (the Yellow Emperor), Zhuan Xu, Emperor Ku, and Sage-kings Yao and Shun.

the most basic structure of early milfoil divination—the trigram images—which became the foundation of Chinese proto-science, may have originated in a primitive religious worldview.

Let us now turn our attention to the second of the three divination manuals, the *Guicang,* a book whose name has yet to be deciphered. Bamboo-slip versions of the *Guicang* were uncovered in 1993 in a Qin dynasty (221–207 BCE) tomb in the village of Wangjiatai. Before this discovery there had existed two incomplete redactions (compilations of fragments from other texts)—one by Yan Kejun (1762–1843) and another by Ma Guohan (1794–1857)—whose authenticity scholars had doubted for various reasons. The Wangjiatai manuscript, although also incomplete, was comprehensive enough to provide evidence that the *Guicang* was the ancestor of the *Zhou Changes.*

Before we can analyze this evidence, it will be necessary to look at another major archaeological discovery. In 1973 a silk manuscript version of the *Zhou Changes,* dating to about 190 BCE, was unearthed at Mawangdui village. The main difference between the Mawangdui manuscript and the received text of the *Zhou Changes* was the order of the hexagrams. In the silk manuscript version, the sequence is based on a regular combination of each hexagram's component trigrams. Essentially, it is a sixty-four-item sequence composed of eight groups of eight hexagrams, each group of which shares the same top trigram and the same order of bottom trigrams. In the received tradition, the sixty-four hexagrams also have a discernible logic, but that logic is based on line transformations and their textual content rather than on trigram configurations.

When the hexagram names of the silk manuscript version of the *Zhou Changes* are compared with the names in the received version, there are numerous inconsistencies. In fact, thirty-three of the sixty-four characters forming hexagram names are different from those of the received text (although more than half of these are simply phonetic loans, like substituting "knot" for "not"). With all these differences, it is significant that the hexagram symbols and names of the silk manuscript *Zhou Changes* and those of the Wangjiatai *Guicang* are a much closer match. This tells us that the *Guicang* had already been using the same sixty-four hexagram names before the *Zhou Changes* became the orthodox book of divination.

Furthermore, the close relationship of the two manuscripts is also a clue that the divination procedure of the *Guicang* was derived from trigrams, since the silk manuscript was organized by trigrams. Not surprisingly, close textual analysis of the Wangjiatai manuscript reveals that the words of some verses correspond to the trigrammatic structure of the hexagram they accompany. For example, the thunder god conducts a divination in the text of the hexagram composed of the trigram for thunder over the trigram for heaven; and the Fire Emperor battles with the Yellow Emperor in the hexagram composed of the trigram for heaven over the trigram for fire. Let us now return to the divination ceremony conducted by the ducal son Chong'er. The use of the thunder trigram as the basis for the inauspicious reading probably indicates that it was based on *Guicang* methodology. The fragmented text of the Yu hexagram in the Wangjiatai manuscript does indeed have an ominous tone: "*Beibei* call the yellow birds; neglected are those lush burial grounds."

I noted previously that the template for the texts of hexagram statements in the *Zhou Changes* was very similar to that of the oracle bone ceremony. However, *Guicang* hexagram statements are much more like those in the oracle bone texts than are the statements in texts of the *Zhou Changes*. They record the diviner's name and the charge—the reason for which the divination ceremony is conducted, which is never the case in the Zhou divination manual. The template for *Guicang* hexagram statements is as follows:

1. A famous personage "cracks bones" about an important matter.
2. Then a particular diviner or shaman "casts lots" about it.
3. Finally the diviner makes a prognostication.

Here are examples from the Wangjiatai manuscript:

161666: *Mingyi* says: In antiquity, Prince Qi of Xia cracked bones about mounting a flying dragon to ascend heaven, and cast lots divining. . . .*

---

*These statements are incomplete due to damage of the bamboo slips that record them. For an explanation of the numbers that precede each example, see pp. 85–86.

616161: *Juan* says: In antiquity, the Yin king cracked bones about whether or not the state would have misfortune. Then he had Shaman Xian cast lots by milfoil. Wu Xian divined, saying: "Inauspicious." He rolled out his mat and cast toward the stream, then rolled it out northward and made sacrifice of a female. . . .

616616: *Lao* says: In antiquity, Chiyou cracked bones about smelting the five weapons. Then he had Scarlet cast lots. . . .

These statements do not actually record a dual shell and milfoil rite, because the word for "crack-making" had become the generic word for "divining." We know this because redacted versions of the hexagram statements replace "cracked bones" with "consulted the milfoil." Here is an example: "In antiquity, Jie consulted the milfoil about attacking Tang and had lots cast. Yinghuo said: 'Inauspicious. There is no advantage in going into battle; the only advantage is being in one's proper place.'"

Not only is the ritual format of the *Guicang* different from that of the *Zhou Changes*, so is the content. Whereas the verses of the *Zhou Changes* remain firmly rooted in the realistic society of Zhou dynasty China, *Guicang* verses sing of sage kings of old, legendary emperors, and mythical creatures. In one case, Gun, the father of the Great Yu, divined about controlling the floods. Chiyou, the tribal ruler who battled the Yellow Emperor and lost, appears once. Other divine diviners include Nü Wa—who formed humans out of yellow clay, Hou Yi—the great archer who shot the sun, Huang Di—the Yellow Emperor, He Bo—the god of the Yellow River, Chang E—the goddess of the moon, Feng Long—the god of thunder, and even Shang Di himself.

Historical figures also appear, which is more reminiscent of the hexagram texts of the *Zhou Changes*. Prince Qi, son of the Great Yu, is the diviner in at least six hexagram statements. Finally, as we have seen, Jie, the last king of the Xia dynasty, divines about attacking Tang, the founder of the Shang dynasty. These references to historical figures are not concrete records of events but citations of idealized moments in the ancient history of China: the overthrow of kings, the founding of new dynasties, and the maintenance of existing reigns.

The texts of the *Guicang* are terse and abstruse when compared to the *Zhou Changes,* whose lines display a tremendous range of realistic human experience and emotion. These distinctions are important clues to the process by which divination ritual must have evolved into metaphysical deliberation. At the very least, the richness of the Zhou text, as opposed to the formulaic terseness of the Shang book of divination, indicates that, by the time the *Zhou Changes* had achieved a stable form, divination had left the confines of the ancestral temple and entered the courtly domain of the nobleman.

One important objective of this chapter was a survey of pre-Qin historical and ritual texts to see just what is and is not known about turtle and milfoil divination procedures before the *Zhou Changes* became the orthodox divination manual. In the course of my presenting early clues and tracing them through the ages to determine how divination evolved, the reader should have perceived that the Chinese slowly began to distance themselves from the world of ancestral spirits and started perceiving the divinatory task as a fathoming of the cosmos. This marked the beginning of metaphysical speculation, whose crowning achievement in ancient China was the commentary tradition that attached itself to the *Zhou Changes.* The next chapter will therefore begin with an analysis of the philosophical tradition that grew up around the divination manual, which eventually propelled the manual and its commentaries to the honorable position of "first of the classics."

CHAPTER 3

The *Zhouyi*, or *Zhou Changes*

According to tradition, the origin of the *Zhou Changes* was "at the hand of three sages, in the time of three epochs." That is to say, the legendary sage-king Fuxi drew the eight trigrams, King Wen of Zhou doubled the trigrams to form the sixty-four hexagrams, and Confucius composed the commentaries. Modern scholars do not normally concern themselves with the question of authorship because there is no way it can be resolved without a great deal of speculation. All we know for sure is that the divinatory text achieved its final form sometime in the Western Zhou period (1046–771 BCE), and the commentary tradition that followed is closely related to Confucius. In fact, the early association of the *Zhou Changes* with Confucius is probably what guaranteed its transmission through the ages. Without a basic understanding of this seminal text, it would not be possible to gain a true understanding of Chinese divination. I have therefore reserved this chapter for outlining facets of the text that are fundamental to an understanding of its traditional use as a divination manual and its influence on subsequent systems of divination. I will begin by describing the content of the book and conclude with an in-depth analysis of stalk-casting methodology and the phenomenon of line change.

The Text of the Zhou Changes

As outlined in the background information, hexagrams are formed of six linear symbols, each of which is a broken *yin* line (symbolized by the number "6") or an unbroken *yang* line (symbolized by "9"), both of which are characterized as "old."* The six lines of the hexagram are

---

* Lines are designated either "young" or "old," depending on their propensity to change.

called the beginning (bottom) line, line 2, line 3, line 4, line 5, and the top line. Each hexagram has a name and a corresponding hexagram statement, and each line has a corresponding line statement. The lines are referenced by their position in the linear hierarchy and by their numerological value. Thus, an old *yin* line in the fourth position from the bottom of a hexagram is called the "6 in the 4th place." Only the first two hexagrams, Qian and Kun, have six identical lines—six unbroken *yang* lines in the case of Qian, and six broken *yin* lines in the case of Kun. So, besides the six line statements for each hexagram, there is also an extra statement called "All Nines" for Qian and "All Sixes" for Kun. These two "All" statements are used when all lines of a hexagram change into their opposite. The complete text of hexagram 1, Qian, is recorded in table 5.

It might be useful here to compare the general template appearing in table 5 with that of the oracle bone divination procedure outlined in chapter 2 (see pp. 29–31). The crack in the bone or shell ("like a

TABLE 5. THE QIAN HEXAGRAM

Line	Omen	Counsel	Prognostication
Hexagram Statement		Your primary plea is heard. A good omen.	
Bottom Nine	Hiding dragon.	Do not use this omen.	
2nd Nine	See the dragon rising in the fields.	It is time to see the great one.	
3rd Nine	The nobleman is vigorous all day and wary by night.	Omen of danger.	No harm will come.
4th Nine	Now it springs up from the deep.		No harm will come.
5th Nine	The dragon flies in the skies.	It is time to see the great one.	
Top Nine	Setting dragon.		There will be problems.
All Nines	See the dragon group without a head.		There will be good fortune.

mountain overhanging"), which elicited the reading by the diviner ("there was a chief who led a raid") was replaced by the omen text in the *Zhou Changes*. The counsel that was sought in the shell-cracking ceremony was not recorded on the shell ("you will gain from opposing the bandits"), but often appears in the *Zhou Changes* text. Finally, the prognostication verse normally appears in both ("it will rain on a 9-stem day").

Although I will explain stalk-casting in more detail in the section below, at this juncture it might be helpful for the reader to know a bit more about the significance of the numerical symbolization to which I just referred. The numbers themselves originate from the manipulation of the milfoil stalks. As I said, the value of 9 represents the old *yang* line, while the value of 6 represents the old *yin* line. An *old* line is one that is about to transform into its opposite, just like all living things change as they get old. *Young* lines, on the other hand, do not transform; they are symbolized by the number 7 (young *yang*) and 8 (young *yin*). It is the concept of the "changing line" that distinguishes the *Zhou Changes* from its predecessors. Whereas the *Guicang* had only sixty-four hexagram symbols with sixty-four accompanying texts (see examples on p. 37), the *Zhou Changes* has sixty-four hexagram symbols and sixty-four accompanying hexagram statements in addition to 384 separate line statements. By the time there are records to give us our first picture of just how the *Zhou Changes* was consulted, the practice of divining by the changing line had been fully implemented. By then, two hexagrams were being derived for a divination ceremony—the root hexagram resulted from the original manipulation of the milfoil stalks, and the derivative hexagram resulted from the transformation of any *old* lines from the root hexagram into their opposite, thus forming a new hexagram. As seen below (pp. 55–56), the auspice of the divined situation could be determined from either of the two hexagram statements, or one or more of the line statements of either hexagram. The permutations of significance afforded by this multivalent system are seemingly countless.

Looking closely at hexagram and line statements from the *Zhou Changes*, the reader will be struck by the vast difference in content and disposition of this text as compared to that of the *Guicang*. In order to make sense of its great complexity, I have divided the contents of the many hexagram and line statements of the *Zhou Changes* into four categories: (1) records of actual events, (2) images that symbolize human affairs, (3) counsels for proper human behavior, and (4) prognostications.

ACTUAL EVENTS

Referencing a famous past event is the least ambiguous way to indicate an ominous statement in a divination ritual. A diviner encountering such a text is very clear of the outcome being forecast. "He loses his cattle in Yi" (5th Six, hexagram 56) recalls the tale of King Hai, ancestor of the Shang kings, who was murdered in the country of Youyi where he had been grazing his livestock. Other stories are just as clear, but the persona can no longer be identified: "They bagged three foxes in the hunt and got bronze arrowheads" (2nd Nine, hexagram 40). Still other stories have obscure origins and judgments that are not easy to discern: "He serves neither king nor feudal lord. Higher still does his service go" (Top Nine, hexagram 18).

SYMBOLIC IMAGES

Things and events that act as metaphors can also indicate good or ill fortune: "A dried-up willow sprouts a new limb. An old man gets a young wife" (2nd Nine, hexagram 28). Some statements are allegorical: "The one-eyed can still see, and the lame can still walk. But if you walk on the tail of a tiger, you will be eaten" (3rd Six, hexagram 10).

COUNSEL STATEMENTS

Since these speeches offer direct guidance to the person consulting the oracle, their intent is usually transparent: "You will gain nothing for three years" (Top Six, hexagram 29). Sometimes the intent of the counsel is clear, even though its specific direction may be metaphorical: "With this omen you may cross the river. Don't go far, or your companions will be left behind" (2nd Nine, hexagram 11). Some counsel statements, on the other hand, need a setting to clarify: "This omen is of no use to the lowborn" (Top Six, hexagram 7) is preceded by: "The great lords have the mandate to found states and sire clans." The majority of counsel statements are formulaic: "To go on a journey will bring regret" (3rd Nine, hexagram 31), "Now is the time to ford the great river" (hexagram statement, hexagram 42), and "Now is the time to see the great one" (hexagram statement, hexagram 45).

PROGNOSTICATIONS

These are statements that judge portent, and such language is almost always attached to one of the other categories of language. What might be intrinsic in an event, a symbol, or a counsel becomes extrinsic in the prognosis given by these statements. For example, "The elder brother leads the troops; the younger carts the bodies. Omen of misfortune" (5th Six, hexagram 7). This is the most formulaic language in the *Zhou Changes* and includes such words as "regret," "danger," and "harm" as forecasts of misfortune. If good fortune is predicted, words such as "favorable" or "happiness" are used, in addition to "auspicious." Prognostication language, being the most generic of all terminology in such manuals, does not differ that much between the *Zhou Changes* and the *Guicang*.

It is considerably easier to discuss the development of the commentary convention of the *Zhou Changes* because there are numerous historical texts that quote hexagram and line statements. The earliest records of divination by milfoil occurred some four centuries after the founding of the Zhou dynasty. As the dynasty progressed, the power of the nobility slowly began to eclipse that of the king. The use of divination, originally a royal prerogative, spread from the capital to the fiefdoms and permeated all of literate society. By the end of the Spring and Autumn period (722-484 BCE), even landless gentry—those without fiefs—were casting the milfoil for everything from making medical prognoses to selecting auspicious days for travel. The text of the *Zhou Changes* was so widely known by then that speakers could allude to particular lines, and listeners would recognize them. This familiarity led to the ever-increasing use of the text to support arguments. Eventually lines were being quoted out of context by those who needed revered texts on which to base their moral instruction. This moralizing slowly began to influence everyone's understanding of the *Zhou Changes* so that much of the original meaning was forgotten. The original divination text had become a book of rhetoric. At this time, a cultured gentleman could sing verses from the *Classic of Odes* to embellish his stories, quote lines from the *Spring and Au-*

tumn Annals to teach the lessons of history, and relate omens from the *Changes* to speculate about the future. The following example from the *Zuo Commentary* will show how far the transformation had progressed.

In 545 BCE, a treaty was formed between various states so that the larger would protect the smaller. The smaller states were required to periodically send emissaries to the larger states to swear allegiance. The State of Zheng sent an official named Youji to the State of Chu, but he was turned back at the border. Chu claimed the treaty required a visit by the ruler of the state, not a mere servant. Youji made this report:

> The ruler of Chu will soon perish. Instead of cultivating a virtuous government, he is greedy and blind in his conduct toward the nobles. Will it be possible for him to continue long? The *Zhou Changes,* under Fu ䷗ changing to Yi ䷚ says, "He loses his way home. Misfortune." Such is the case with the ruler of Chu. He seeks what he desires, but abandons what is essential, so there is no place to return to [the meaning of the hexagram name, Fu]. This is what is meant by "losing his way home." How can he not meet with misfortune?

The Top 6 of hexagram Fu, an old *yin* line, changes to a *yang* line to form the hexagram Yi. Thus the statement of the top line of Fu is the basis for Youji's comment. However, there is no record that stalks were cast to derive this line, so is it a prognostication or simply a shrewd observation? The *Spring and Autumn Annals* reports that the ruler of Chu died some months later. So Youji's comments were indeed a prediction, but one apparently determined by mental acuity rather than divine power.

The use of the divination text by a growing bureaucratic class without recourse to divination is the setting for increasingly philosophical interpretations of the *Zhou Changes.* The Warring States period was the blossoming of the "hundred schools" when philosophical reasoning flourished. As theories were debated in the intellectual centers of the various states, esteemed texts like the *Zhou Changes* were reinterpreted in line with the new ways of thinking. Moralists concentrated on ethical issues they found in the social content of the text. And mystics were interested in the symbolic relations between the linear symbols.

Thanks to the discovery of the silk manuscript *Zhou Changes* at Mawangdui, which reflects a somewhat different school of thought from that which eventually coalesced into the classic of the received tradition, we have a candid view of a different commentary tradition that will help clarify the stages of development. The silk manuscript contained five sections, only one commentary of which is also represented in the received tradition, the "Appended Statements," although the two versions differ considerably. Some scholars believe that the silk manuscript "Appended Statements" betrays a Daoist bias. Conversely, another commentary in the Mawangdui text, the "Properties of the Changes," presents a decidedly Confucian stance. The remaining commentaries, "Several Disciples Ask," "Essentials," and "Masters Mu He and Zhao Li," for the most part all use the dialogue format, some between Confucius and his disciples and some between other interlocutors. Especially in the content of the last commentary—the questions of the two unknown thinkers, Mu He and Zhao Li—the text of the *Zhou Changes* is quoted to explain moral precepts.

One of the most interesting passages in the silk manuscript, occurring in the "Essentials" commentary, is a conversation between Confucius and his disciple Zi Gong. Here, Confucius seems concerned about his reputation because he has taken up the practice of divination in his old age. When criticized by Zi Gong, who assumed that Confucius was a teacher of ethics and not a diviner, his teacher admits to having practiced divining but explains his purposes as follows:

> With the appraisals [line statements] if you do not apprehend the numbers, then you are just being a shaman; with the numbers, if you do not apprehend what is virtuous, then you are just being a diviner. The stalk-counting of diviners and shamans is getting there but has not yet arrived; they enjoy what they do but are nevertheless wrong. If later generations of scholars doubt me, will it be because of the *Changes*? I seek only its virtue. I tread the same path as the diviners and shamans, but our destinations are different.

While there was much discussion in scholarly circles in the twentieth century concerning the extent of Confucius' role in the commentary tradition, this passage from a hitherto unknown text seems to be saying that Confucius believed that the mere understanding of the mystical character of the text was inadequate unless one attended equally to the moral dimensions of the statements.

This interesting evaluation of the *Zhou Changes* is clearly the prevailing attitude that produced the seven commentaries (in ten sections) that we know from the received tradition as the *Ten Wings*: (1) *Commentary on the Hexagram Statement* I, II; (2) *Commentary on the Images* I, II; (3) *Commentary on the Appended Statements* I, II; (4) *Wenyan*; (5) *Trigram Explanation Commentary*; (6) *Hexagram Sequence*; and (7) *Hexagram Relationships*. Let us now take a brief look at the four most important of these essays.

1. "Commentary on the Hexagram Statement"
   In the "Commentary on the Hexagram Statement," each hexagram name is explained by providing a moral context. Then, using various linear relationships, the good or bad fortune of each hexagram is determined from its unique structure of lines. The hexagram symbol consists of six positions, half of which (the first, third, and fifth places, counting from the bottom) are described as superior, and half of which (the second, fourth, and sixth places) are described as inferior. When a *yang* line occupies a superior position, or when a *yin* line occupies an inferior position, order and therefore good fortune is suggested. With this in mind, hexagram 63, "After Crossing" ䷾ is considered the most balanced in the entire *Zhou Changes* because all lines occupy their proper position. Lines whose strength does not match their station represent disorder and thus misfortune, which is the case with hexagram 64, "Before Crossing" ䷿, where each of the six positions is occupied by the improper line.

   The "Commentary on the Hexagram Statement" also analyzes hexagrams according to their composite trigrams. The corresponding lines of each trigram in a given hexagram (lines 1 and 4, lines 2 and 5, lines 3 and 6) attract each other if they are occupied by symbols of *opposite* character. In other words, a *yin* line in position 1 of the lower trigram is attracted to a *yang* line in position 4 of the upper trigram. This is

interpreted as auspicious. Finally, the second and fifth places in a hexagram, by virtue of their central position in each trigram, are interpreted as the hexagram's rulers.

For example, hexagram 37, "Family" ䷤, is composed of the trigram for wood over the trigram for fire. The hexagram statement and its commentary read as follows:

> Hexagram statement: Family. A good omen for a girl.
> "Commentary": Family. The correct place of the woman is inside; the correct place of the man is outside. That man and woman have their proper places is the great model of heaven and earth. In home and family there are strict rulers called the parents. When the father is a father and the son a son, when the elder brother is an elder brother and the younger brother a younger brother, when the husband is a husband and the wife a wife, this is the proper way of the family. When the family is proper, then all under heaven is secure.

This passage is a good example of a commentary derived from the concept of the hexagram rulers. The lower or inner trigram is ruled by a *yin* line, representing the woman. The upper or outer trigram is ruled by a *yang* line, representing the man. The two rulers are opposite in nature, thus they attract each other. Heaven and earth are opposite, with heaven above and earth below. Man and woman are opposite, with man above and woman below. Thus the "Commentary" says, "That man and woman have their proper places is the great model of heaven and earth."

2. "Trigram Explanation Commentary"

The "Trigram Explanation" begins with a terse, metaphysical account of the creation of the hexagrams by sages. Then it discusses the eight trigrams, expanding each of the general trigram categories into as many as twenty distinct terms in correlative categories such as family member, types of animal, direction, season, social status, color, and body part. For example, the trigram *qian* (heaven) correlates with the father, the horse, northwest, early winter, the king, deep red, and the head. Table 6 lists trigram attributes derived mainly from this commentary.

TABLE 6. TRIGRAM ATTRIBUTES

Name	Family	Animal	Direction	Season	Person	Color	Body Part	Misc.
Qian Heaven	father	dragon, horse	north-west	early winter	king	deep red	head	fruit, ice
Kun Earth	mother	cow and calf	south-west	early autumn	the people	black	stomach	cloth, wagon
Zhen Thunder	eldest son	flying dragon	east	spring equinox	young men	dark yellow	feet	bamboo, commands
Kan Water	second son	pig	north	winter solstice	thieves	blood red	ears	wheels, the moon
Gen Mountain	youngest son	dog, rat	north-east	early spring	gate-keepers	—	hands	pebbles, a path
Xun Wood	eldest daughter	hen	south-east	early summer	merchants	white	thigh	plumb and square
Li Fire	second daughter	pheasant, toad, turtle	south	summer solstice	big-bellied men	—	eyes	armor, spear
Dui Lake	youngest daughter	sheep and goat	west	autumn equinox	shaman, concubine	—	mouth	salty

In the "Trigram Explanation" are also collected sayings that explain how the trigrams relate to each other spatially and temporally. One passage names the trigrams in a sequence of pairs—heaven and earth, lake and mountain, fire and water, thunder and wind/wood; this is the origin of the pre-heaven order, sometimes called the Fuxi arrangement (see fig. 6). Another passage is the origin of the post-heaven sequence of trigrams, which was analyzed in some detail in chapter 2 (where it was called the "God emerges" passage). This order forms the basis of *fengshui* auspice computation.

3. "Commentary on the Images"

    The "Commentary on the Images" divides each hexagram into its component trigrams and deduces the meaning of the hexagram from its trigrams, finally drawing sociological conclusions based upon that deduction. For example, the trigram for thunder over the trigram for water forms hexagram 40, "Deliverance" ䷧. The "Commentary on the Images" for this hexagram's statement reads as follows: "After thunder, rain is produced. This is Deliverance. Thus the lord forgives errors and pardons crimes." In other words, when the heavens are sufficiently dark and oppressive, lightning strikes, thunder roars, and rain falls. In the "Trigram Explanation" commentary, the trigram for water is correlated with the thief, whereas thunder is correlated with decisiveness and the giving of commands (see table 6). In addition, the name of the hexagram literally means "to untie," so the "Commentary on the Images" hypothesizes in these two trigrams the image of the ruler issuing a command that the thief be released.

    The correlation of natural image to social image is an important one in ancient Chinese thought. We see it in many hexagrams of the *Zhou Changes*. It is even more common in the *Classic of Odes:* "Deep rolls the thunder beneath the southern hills. / Why, oh why, must you always be away?" These are examples of a holistic worldview that does not separate the human realm from the realm of nature.

4. "Commentary on the Appended Statements," or "Great Commentary"

The most important commentary of the *Ten Wings* is called the "Commentary on the Appended Statements," or the "Great Commentary," and dates no later than 175 BCE. This work, unlike the other *Wings*, does not consist of line-by-line or hexagram-specific commentaries but is an essay about the nature of the *Zhou Changes*. Concepts in the "Appended Statements" are tantamount to a metaphysics of change.

The term *yi* means "change" (but can also mean "easy"), which may specifically refer to the change of one hexagram into another. According to the "Appended Statements," the system of the sixty-four hexagrams is a model of the cosmos (heaven and earth). In this context, change is discussed from two different perspectives—change in the natural world, the macrocosm, and change in the hexagrams of the *Zhou Changes*, the microcosm. This concept of change can be subdivided into ordered change and random change. Ordered change is alternation—the reversal of bipolar opposites. We see it in the *Zhou Changes* as the alternation of *yin* and *yang* lines; it occurs in nature as the alternation of day and night. Random change, on the other hand, is chance. In the *Zhou Changes* we see it in the random appearance of the changing line; in the real world it is manifested in the sudden appearance of omens and the occurrence of supernatural phenomena.

Time is also a factor of change. In the "Appended Statements" time is presented as a function of alternation and progression, just as the seasons alternate as the months progress throughout the year. On the microcosmic level, the hexagram is perceived as a model of seasonal time. Alternation here is manifested, for example, by a *yin* line encroaching upon a *yang* line, which mimics the change from hot to cold seasons, the change from day to night, the change from youth to maturity, and so on. In the stalk-casting ritual, the microcosm and the macrocosm merge. As the hexagram progresses from the bottom upward, replicating organic growth, each line captures a possible development in the world outside the diviner. So the chance appearance of a given line in a given position, which resulted in a given omen, was equivalent to a real-life occurrence of a supernatural event or portent. The hexagram omen, as such, was a microcosmic model of a unique moment in the life of the inquirer.

The philosophers who pondered the mysteries of the *Changes* in the final centuries of the Zhou dynasty and the first century of the Han had a difficult task before them: to take a collection of oracular texts and develop it into a coherent system of thought. In their attempt to make sense of a largely forgotten tradition, they managed to create a metaphysics that explained the order in the universe. They were so successful that the theories proposed in the "Great Commentary" became the basis of Chinese philosophy down to the present. In 136 BCE, Emperor Wu of the Han dynasty established academic chairs for each of the five Confucian texts: the *Changes, Odes, Documents, Rites,* and *Spring and Autumn Annals.* Henceforth these texts were called *jing,* or classics, and became the canon or curriculum of the Han Academy. From this point on, the *Zhouyi,* or *Zhou Changes,* was also known as the *Yijing,* or *Classic of Changes.*

The Methodology of Stalk-casting

The only authoritative record of stalk-casting procedure in the classical tradition occurs in a passage of the "Appended Statements" commentary known as the Great Extension. Part of that important passage reads as follows:

> The number of the Great Extension is 50, of which 49 are used. Separating into two lots represents twoness. Suspending one represents threeness. Counting off by fours represents the four seasons. Returning the remainder to the fingers represents the leap month. Within five months there is a second leap month, so a second remainder is placed between the fingers. Heaven's numbers are five, and earth's numbers are five. When these five positions combine forces, each number has a complement. Heaven's num-

bers total 25, and earth's numbers total 30. Together they equal 55. This is how change and transformation arise so that the ghosts and spirits move.

This passage presupposes that numbers underlie the operations of the phenomenal world and discusses how the stalks can be manipulated so that the diviner may use those numbers to look into the future. That is, by knowing how these numbers change and transform, we can know how the spirits move. The use here of the term "ghosts and spirits" might seem unusual in a discussion of numerological processes. However, the numbers might be thought of as numerical equivalents of metaphysical entities like star spirits (especially the "nine stars," but also including the five "moving stars," or planets) or other manifestations of natural forces, such as celestial and earthly conjunctions (especially of the heaven stems and earth branches). See the discussion below of Compass School *fengshui* and fate-calculation. I will now examine relevant portions of the passage line by line with the specific intent of understanding how the stalk-casting ritual proceeded.

"The number of the Great Extension is 50, of which 49 are used." Several lines later in the passage the "Appended Statements" describes the numbers 1–10 as either heavenly (odd numbers) or earthly (even numbers). The Great Extension, therefore, is the expansion of the heavenly and earthly numbers to their full limit. However, the number used for divination is forty-nine, not fifty (or fifty-five, the sum of all heavenly and earthly numbers). Forty-nine is the only number whose manipulation in the manner discussed below can result in the final calculations of six, seven, eight, or nine—the numbers that correspond to the lines of the hexagrams.*

---

*The mathematical formula for deriving the final calculation is as follows: $49 \div 2 = A$, $(49-A)$. $(A-1) \div 4 = B$, with remainder C. $(49-A) \div 4 = D$, with remainder E. $1+C+E=F$. Thus, $F=5$ or 9. $(49-F) \div 2 = G$, $[(49-F)-G]$. $(G-1) \div 4 = H$, with remainder I. $[(49-F)-G] \div 4 = J$, with remainder K. $1+I+K=L$. Thus, $L=4$ or 8. $(49-L) \div 2 = M$, $[(49-L)-M]$. $(M-1) \div 4 = N$, with remainder O. $[(49-L)-M] \div 4 = P$, with remainder Q. Thus, $(N+P)=6, 7, 8,$ or 9.

"Separating into two lots represents twoness." Taking the forty-nine stalks in the hands, divide them into two approximately equal bunches. The bunch in the left hand symbolizes heaven, or *yang*, and the bunch in the right hand symbolizes earth, or *yin*.

"Suspending one represents threeness." Take one stalk from the right bunch and place it between the little finger and ring finger of the left hand. This symbolizes humankind. Thus, the triad of heaven, earth, and man is complete.

"Counting off by fours represents the four seasons." Remove the stalks in the left hand by groups of four. Then do the same with the stalks in the right hand. Generally, three to five groups of four stalks will be removed from each hand in each step of the process. The groups of four stalks symbolize the four seasons. Removing them indicates the projection of time.

"Returning the remainder to the fingers represents the leap month. Within five months there is a second leap month, so a second remainder is placed between the fingers." After stalks are removed by fours, in each hand there will be one, two, three, or four stalks remaining. Place the remainder from the left hand between the ring finger and the middle finger of the left hand. Place the remainder from the right hand between the middle finger and the index finger of the left hand. The leftover stalks symbolize the days that accumulate during the passing of years to form a leap month, which occurs approximately every thirty-two months. Thus, in any given five-year period there can be two leap months.

With this statement, the description of the general stalk-casting procedure is complete. However, the detailed steps for deriving a hexagram line are not outlined in the Great Extension passage. So, I will complete the picture of stalk manipulation by describing the procedure as it is traditionally conducted. After stalks have been removed by fours from the heaven bunch and the earth bunch, the stalks remaining in each hand follow a certain pattern: four stalks will remain in each hand, one stalk will remain in the left hand and three stalks in the right hand, two stalks will remain in each hand, or three stalks will remain in the left hand and one stalk in the right. When these stalks are placed in the proper digital interstices, and when they are added to the one reserved stalk that represented human beings, there will be either a total of *five* or *nine* stalks reserved in the left hand. Put these stalks aside. This is the first step of the stalk-counting procedure, which is called the "first change."

There will now be either forty-four or forty stalks left from the original forty-nine. Divide these stalks arbitrarily into two equal bunches just like before. Take one stalk from the right bunch and place it between the little finger and ring finger of the left hand. Count off the left, or heaven, bunch by fours until only one, two, three, or four stalks remain. Place this remainder between the ring finger and the middle finger of the left hand. Move to the right, or earth, bunch and count off by fours until only one, two, three, or four remain. Place this remainder between the middle finger and the index finger of the left hand.

After stalks have been removed by fours, the stalks remaining in both hands will also follow a certain pattern: if the left hand holds one stalk, the right hand will hold two stalks; if the left hand holds two stalks, the right hand will hold one stalk; if the left hand holds three stalks, the right hand will hold four stalks; and if the left hand holds four stalks, the right hand will hold three stalks. Combined with the one stalk between the little finger and ring finger that began the second procedure, there will be either *four* or *eight* stalks reserved in the left hand. Put these stalks aside. This is the second step of the stalk-counting procedure, which is called the "second change."

There will now be thirty-two, thirty-six, or forty stalks remaining from the original forty or forty-four. Separate them into two equal bunches. Beginning with the right bunch, take one stalk and place it between the little finger and ring finger of the left hand. Then count off by fours as in the previous steps. After stalks have been removed by fours, the stalks remaining in each hand will follow the same pattern as with the second change: two and one, one and two, three and four, or four and three. Combined with the one stalk between the little finger and ring finger that began the third procedure, there will now also be a total of either *four* or *eight* stalks reserved in the left hand. Put these stalks aside. This is called the "third change."

Now that the three changes have occurred, it is possible to determine the first line of the hexagram. There are various methods for deriving the line from the three changes, but the most well known is called the "quartering-stalk method." In this process the character of the line is determined from the number of stalks counted out by four during the third change. That number will be twenty-four, twenty-eight, thirty-two, or thirty-six. We then divide this number by four to determine the passage of seasons:

- 28 stalks ÷ 4 = 7, the number of young *yang*
- 32 stalks ÷ 4 = 8, the number of young *yin*
- 36 stalks ÷ 4 = 9, the number of old *yang*
- 24 stalks ÷ 4 = 6, the number of old *yin*

As we saw previously, the term *young* is used to describe a hexagram line that does not change. The term *old* describes a line that will change into its opposite and form the second hexagram of a casting session. Thus, old *yang* will change into a *yin* line, and old *yin* will change into a *yang* line. The entire three-step procedure is repeated five more times to obtain a total of six lines for the completed hexagram.

The Song dynasty Neo-Confucian scholar, Zhu Xi (1130–1200), basing his work on the divination examples recorded in the *Zuo Commentary* and *Discourses on the States*, determined that there were seven different ways to divine according to the number of changing lines in a hexagram. These were:

1. If there are no changing lines, the divination is based on the hexagram statement of the root hexagram.
2. If there is one changing line, the divination is based on the text of the changing line of the root hexagram.
3. If there are two changing lines, the divination is based on the text of the two changing lines of the root hexagram, and the upper of the two lines is the ruler.
4. If there are three changing lines, the divination is based on the hexagram statements of the root hexagram and the changed hexagram, and the root hexagram is the ruler.
5. If there are four changing lines, the divination is based on the text of the two unchanging lines of the changed hexagram, with the lower line as the ruler.
6. If there are five changing lines, the divination is based on the text of the unchanging line of the changed hexagram.

7. If all six lines are changing, use the two "All" line statements of the Qian and Kun hexagrams. Refer also to the hexagram statement of the changed hexagram.

Zhu Xi authored two influential books on the *Zhou Changes,* the *Original Meaning of the Zhou Changes* (a commentary on the original text and the commentaries) and the *Introduction to the Study of the Changes* (a discussion of the practice of divination). This passage comes from the latter work.

The concept of line change was first addressed philosophically in the "Appended Statements" commentary: "The sages created the hexagrams from their observation of the world and then appended statements to illuminate good and bad fortune. As the hard and the soft push each other, change and transformation occur. Thus 'auspicious' and 'inauspicious' represent gain and loss; 'regret' and 'harm' represent grief and worry. Change and transformation are characterized by progression and retrogression." The *yin* and *yang* lines—characterized here as soft and hard—displace each other as one changes or transforms into the other. Thus, when an old *yin* line (6) changes into a young *yang* line (7), this is an image of progression. When an old *yang* line (9) transforms into a young *yin* line (8), this is an image of retrogression. In the terminology of the commentary, change is the "movement" from a state of disequilibrium (changing) to one of stability (changed). When balance has been achieved, knowledge is gained: "The line and its image move from within; good fortune and misfortune appear externally." When the root and derivative hexagrams have been determined, the proper hexagram and line statements then express the auspice of the situation in the phenomenal world.

As the theory of line and hexagram change developed in the Han dynasty and afterward, it became more and more methodical. Lines and trigram or hexagram images served increasingly as the symbolic representation of mathematical and calendrical patterns rather than as a medium for philosophical abstraction. Such thinkers as Jing Fang (77–37 BCE) and Yu Fan (164–233 CE) were eventually grouped in the school known as "image and number," to distinguish them from the "meaning and principle" school represented by Wang Bi (226–249). Wang's *Commentary on the Zhou Changes* is considered the first philosophical commentary on the text and set the standard for orthodox scholarship until the Song dynasty. The works of Jing Fang and Yu Fan, on the other hand, were the foundation upon which Chinese alchemy was constructed in the third century. It is the school of image and number that was to have a lasting influence on the development of Chinese divination.

Hexagram Conversion

Any single hexagram can convert into any of the other sixty-three hexagrams by the change or transformation of one to six lines. But on a larger scale, individual hexagrams or groups of hexagrams can be visualized as the generator of more complex systems of hexagrams by virtue of line change. This process is known as "hexagram conversion," as opposed to the "changed hexagram" (otherwise known as the derivative hexagram). For example, hexagrams 1 and 2, those made up entirely of *yang* and *yin* lines, respectively, were understood to change into six offspring hexagrams (those corresponding to the doubled trigrams thunder, water, mountain, wood, fire, and lake). These six hexagram children (older, middle, and younger brother; older, middle, and younger sister) can then change into the remaining fifty-six hexagrams.

I will now outline several esoteric systems derived from line change and hexagram conversion, many of which are still in common use.

INTERLOCKING, LATERALLY LINKED, AND CUMULATIVE TRANSFORMED HEXAGRAMS

Interlocking hexagrams are pairs of hexagrams in which the second hexagram is formed from the first, based on two trigrams derived from the interior lines of the first. The interior, or nuclear, trigrams are lines 2 through 4 and lines 3 through 5, counting from the bottom. For example, from the nuclear trigrams of hexagram 30, Li ☲ , can be derived the interlocking counterpart, hexagram 28, Da Guo ☱. Laterally linked or complementary hexagrams are pairs of hexagrams wherein the individual lines of one are opposite in kind to those of the other. Thus, hexagram 2, Kun, is the complementary hexagram of hexagram 1, Qian. Lines, trigrams, and hexagrams can all have complements. Nuclear trigrams and complementary lines are most commonly used to explain the origin of hexagram and line statements. But they also act as steps in more complex systems of hexagram transformation. That is also the case with cumulative transformation, which is a sequential transformation of several hexagrams from one parent hexagram such that each transformed hexagram accumulates the changed line of its predecessor (see immediately below, where Qian is the parent hexagram).

EIGHT PALACES

To the Han dynasty diviner Jing Fang is attributed the arrangement of the sixty-four hexagrams called the Eight Palaces. This sequence of hexagrams is formed of eight systematic groups of eight hexagrams in the following array. Each of the eight palace groups begins with one of the eight pure hexagrams (those composed of the doubled trigrams), in the following order of the eight trigrams: heaven, thunder, water, mountain, earth, wood, fire, and lake. To form the second through the sixth hexagrams in the sequence of eight, a cumulative transformation is conducted. Thus, starting with Qian of the first palace, we obtain the following hexagrams (called the first through fifth generations):

☰ ☰ ☰ ☰ ☰ ☰

To obtain the seventh hexagram, take the previous hexagram (the fifth generation, which has undergone the cumulative change to the fifth line), and then conduct a complementary transformation of the fourth line. This is called the "wandering soul" transformation.

☰ ☰

To form the eighth hexagram, take the previous hexagram (which has undergone the wandering soul transformation), and then conduct a complementary transformation of the lower trigram. This is called the "homing soul" transformation.

☰ ☰

These eight hexagrams therefore constitute the first palace:

☰ ☰ ☰ ☰ ☰ ☰ ☰ ☰

Using the same techniques, we can derive the remaining seven palaces. For example, the fifth palace begins with the pure hexagram Kun and is essentially the complement of the first palace:

☷ ☷ ☷ ☷ ☷ ☷ ☷ ☷

As mentioned, the eight palaces accord with the following order of the eight trigrams (and pure hexagrams): heaven, thunder, water, mountain, earth, wood, fire, and lake. This is the order of the "family member" trigrams: father, first son, second son, third son, mother, first daughter, second daughter, and third daughter.

INSERTED STEMS

The technique of "inserting stems" makes use of the two unique Chinese numbering sequences called heaven stems and earth branches (see tables 2 and 3). To insert the stems, the eight trigrams are generally correlated with the heaven stems. In Jing Fang's system in particular, the eight pure hexagrams (representing each of the Eight Palaces) are matched with the heaven stems. Then, in a process known as "inserted branches," the six line positions in each hexagram are matched with the twelve earth branches in a step similar to that in the method of line chronograms below. This step adds a temporal value to each hexagram because the twelve branches represent each of the twelve months and one of the five phases. Table 7 shows how stems and branches are inserted into the pure hexagrams. In this chart the parenthetical phase designations in the top row correspond to the

TABLE 7. INSERTING STEMS AND BRANCHES

Palace/Line	Heaven (metal)	Thunder (wood)	Water (water)	Mountain (earth)	Earth (earth)	Wood (wood)	Fire (fire)	Lake (metal)
Top line	9 K earth	7 K earth	5 A water	3 C wood	10 F fire	8 L water	6 J metal	4 H earth
5th line	9 I metal	7 I metal	5 K earth	3 A water	10 D wood	8 J metal	6 H earth	4 F fire
4th line	9 G fire	7 G fire	5 I metal	3 K earth	10 B earth	8 H earth	6 F fire	4 D wood
3rd line	1 E earth	7 E earth	5 G fire	3 I metal	2 L water	8 F fire	6 D wood	4 B earth
2nd line	1 C wood	7 C wood	5 E earth	3 G fire	2 J metal	8 D wood	6 B earth	4 L water
Bottom line	1 A water	7 A water	5 C wood	3 E earth	2 H earth	8 B earth	6 L water	4 J metal

five-phase value of each of the palaces, whereas the phases indicated in the remainder of the chart correspond to individual lines of the hexagrams. The correlation between palace phase and line phase enables the diviner to apply the rules of production and conquest, which thereby accounts for the determination of auspice. For an application of inserted stems, see the form of divination called Fire Pearl Collection in chapter 5.

WAXING AND WANING QI

The waxing and waning sequence is composed of twelve "sovereign" hexagrams that illustrate the accumulation and dispersion of *qi* during the year. Beginning with hexagram 24, Fu ䷗ (which represents the winter solstice), a cumulative transformation may be conducted to acquire the six hexagrams ending with hexagram 1, Qian:

䷗ ䷒ ䷊ ䷡ ䷫ ䷀

These show the ascent of *yang qi* over the first six months and can be likened to the waxing of the moon from crescent stage to the full moon.

Then, beginning with hexagram 44, Gou ䷫ (which represents the summer solstice), a cumulative transformation may be conducted to acquire the six hexagrams ending with hexagram 2, Kun.

䷀ ䷫ ䷠ ䷋ ䷓ ䷁

These show the displacement by *yin qi* during the remainder of the year and can be likened to the waning cycles of the moon until the stage of the new moon is reached.

HEXAGRAM BREATHS

This method coordinates the sixty-four hexagrams with time in the following manner. Based on the post-heaven sequence of the eight trigrams, hexagrams 29, 30, 51, and 58—the pure hexagrams for water, fire, thunder, and lake—represent the four seasons of winter, summer, spring, and fall (see p. 16). Each line of these four hexagrams corresponds to one of the twenty-four seasonal breaths (fifteen-day divisions of the year). The remaining sixty hexagrams are equally divided among the twelve months. Each hexagram thus corresponds to approximately six days.

LINE CHRONOGRAMS

Line chronograms coordinate each of the six line positions of the Qian and Kun hexagrams with one of the twelve earthly branches indicating time. Beginning from the bottom line of each hexagram, table 8 attaches the branches to the proper line position. Parenthetical numbers are each branch's order in the duo-decimal cycle. Notice that *yang* lines are represented by odd numbers, whereas *yin* lines correspond to even numbers. The twelve lines of these two hexagrams are then the representatives of all the *yin* and *yang* lines of the remaining sixty-two hexagrams; every beginning *yang* line in any hexagram that begins with a *yang* line therefore corresponds to branch A, and every beginning *yin* line in such hexagrams corresponds to H. Similarly, every top *yang* line in the *Zhou Changes* is a K branch, and every top *yin* line is an F branch. In addition to the twelve branches, the twelve pitch-pipe notes, the twelve stations of the ecliptic, and the twenty-eight lunar mansions (zodiacal constellations) are all coordinated with the same twelve lines in order to indicate the rhythm of the twelve double-hours of the day or the twelve months of the year.

The abovementioned techniques are the most important of an enormous and complicated body of *Yi*-style divination procedures that began to develop in the Han dynasty. The concepts of hexagram conversion just described were ostensibly "discovered" by scholars such as Jing Fang rather than "invented." Since such linear relationships supposedly coexisted with the writing of the statement passages, it stands to reason that such hexagram manipulation would be useful for interpreting many of the seemingly unintelligible line statements. At the same time, the concepts could be used to facilitate new forms

TABLE 8. LINE CHRONOGRAMS

Qian	Branch	Kun	Branch
Top 9	K (11)	Top 6	F (6)
5th 9	I (9)	5th 6	D (4)
4th 9	G (7)	4th 6	B (2)
3rd 9	E (5)	3rd 6	L (12)
2nd 9	C (3)	2nd 6	J (10)
Bottom 9	A (1)	Bottom 6	H (8)

of divination. In the pre-Qin period, the main function of line and hexagram conversion in the practice of divination was to enable the diviner to capture the changeability of a particular situation so that the proper fortune could be deduced from the appropriate hexagram or line statement. As the concept of line change developed, the divination event was seen to reveal merely one point in a long sequence of stages. Knowing the sequence enabled the diviner to chart the proper path in the near and distant future based on the current situation. Eventually, the mantic text became secondary to the process as the numerology of the lines and their cosmological import became paramount. This concentration on the mystical character of the text at the expense of the moral quality of its statements is precisely what Confucius seems to have been cautioning against in the above passage from the "Essentials" (see p. 46).

Divination by image and number probably originated in the Neolithic period with the manipulation of colored stones, and flourished in the pre-Qin period with crack-making and stalk-counting. In the Qin and early Han there was substantial development in theory and metaphysical speculation, whereas the later Han dynasty saw a proliferation of schools and movements—most notably the numerological schemes of the image and number school. Unlike the preceding discussion, which was organized chronologically because the evolution of a tradition was paramount, the remainder of the book will proceed thematically by the categories of divination: numerology (divining by counting), augury (divining by interpreting images), and sortilege (divining by choosing). What follows may be thought of as documentation of the most important practical applications of the theories outlined in preceding chapters.

CHAPTER 4
Fengshui, or Tomb and Residential Site Orientation

What we know about the origin of Chinese divination is based almost entirely on artifacts excavated in Neolithic period tombs such as those at Jiahu and Lingjiatan. It is not clear why the turtles were buried with the dead. Some scholars hypothesize that even in the Neolithic period such numinous objects were placed in tombs to be used by the deceased in the afterlife. If that is the case, then the tomb itself might have been the main locus of that posthumous spiritual realm, so the position and configuration of the tomb would have been very important. One of the most essential forms of Chinese divination is the location and orientation of the tomb, called the "nether home" by *fengshui* specialists. Let us take a closer look at a Neolithic grave to see if there is any evidence of this form of divination this early in Chinese culture.

A tomb unearthed in 1987 at the Xishuipo Yangshao culture ruins west of Puyang City in Henan Province contains the earliest image of the dragon ever discovered in China, dating back more than 6,400 years (see fig. 13). This dragon flanks the left side of the skeleton of a man that occupies the upper central chamber of the tomb. To the right of the skeleton is the image of a tiger, and in the center of the tomb is another image that is not as easy to identify. All three figures are outlined in clamshells. Since there are immense Dragon and Tiger constellations flanking the North Star in the Chinese sky (attestable only since the Warring States period), these clamshell figures might represent stellar deities. If so, it is likely that the unidentified shell figure is Beidou (Northern Ladle), the Chinese name for the Big Dipper.

The great macro-constellation called the Cerulean Dragon, which symbolizes the east in Chinese cosmology, is composed of seven

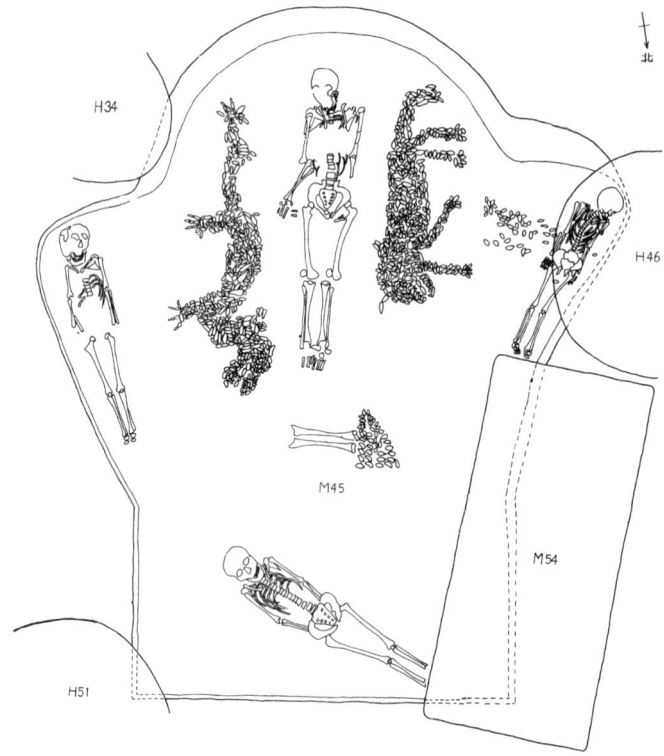

Fig. 13. Neolithic tomb at Xishuipo (after Wenwu *1988, no. 3, p. 4)*

smaller constellations, including the Tail, Heart, Neck, and Horn. The White Tiger is also made of seven smaller constellations, including the Stomach; it symbolizes the west. In the idealized Chinese sky, the Dragon and Tiger both face south. However, in the Xishuipo tomb, both creatures face north, toward the bottom of the illustration. So, if these shell creatures are indeed the Dragon and Tiger of the Chinese sky, looking down into the tomb is actually like looking up into heaven. The tomb illustration is not a mirror image of the sky; it is like a map of the sky. In order for its shell figures to correspond to constellations in the sky, the observer would have to hold it overhead. In so doing, the deceased would effectively be placed precisely in the center of heaven, which is presumably where his spirit dwells.

At least in its use of the dragon and tiger images, the conception that inspired this tomb structure shares the primary symbols of the traditional *fengshui* burial site. So this tomb arrangement might be seen as the first evidence of a proto-*fengshui*. The earliest literary reference to a full-fledged practice of burial *fengshui* does not occur for more than four thousand years after Xishuipo. The *Book of Burial*, attributed to Guo Pu (276–324 CE) but more likely a product of the Tang dynasty (618–907 CE), records the following passage describing mountain burial sites: "The heavenly lights regenerate the site, like rivers returning to the sea, or like the stars revolving around the North Star. It is embraced and protected by the dragon and tiger that receive each other like host and guest." By the Han dynasty, this perception of the cosmos was refined and reproduced throughout the culture in areas as diverse as art motifs and proto-scientific instruments such as the cosmograph.

The earliest textual reference to the practice of what eventually would be called residential *fengshui* comes from the *Classic of Odes*. In a cycle of poems praising the exploits of the illustrious ancestors of the Zhou dynasty, the hero Gong Liu, great-grandson of the millet god, Hou Ji, appears. Chief Liu led an exodus of his people to the fertile lands of Bin in the year 1796 BCE, according to tradition. The poem recounts the founding of his new domain, and this excerpt shows him conducting a geophysical survey:

> Blessed was Chief Liu.
> He measured the breadth and length of the land;
> He measured the shadow and noted the hills,
> Observing the sunshine and shade. (Mao #250)

Liu was measuring the shadow of the gnomon, or sundial, to determine the cardinal directions. Sunshine and shade are the original meanings of the well-known terms *yang* and *yin*, which appear here in one of their earliest textual references. With this information he could determine which side of the hills and valleys received the most sunshine during the winter.

With these two bodies of evidence—archaeological records of Neolithic China and literary records of legendary China—we can already see the general outline of proto-*fengshui*. The orientation of tombs was as important as the orientation of homes, the minimum requirement for either was the determination of direction, and both astronomical and geophysical factors were consulted. It is this last point that demands our further attention. In these two categories lie the origins of what eventually became the two major schools of *fengshui*, the Patterns of Qi School (also known as the Compass School and the Fujian School), and the Forms and Terrain School (also known as the Intuitive School and the Jiangxi School).

The earliest organized school of diviners whose arts may be considered direct antecedents of traditional *fengshui* practices were the *kanyu* masters of the Han dynasty (for an explanation of *kanyu*, see the discussion below). However, due to the loss of the *Golden Chest of Kanyu*, a product of this school, it is difficult to determine the full extent of its theories. Scholars speculate that the *kanyu* masters were proficient in at least two types of divination, one that determined auspicious days and another that divined auspicious directions. Examples of both have been found in Qin dynasty almanacs (see below). The locus classicus for the term is the astronomy chapter of *Huainanzi*: "On the *kanyu* the male is slowly moved in order to know the female" (3.29). From its context here, it is clear that some type of astronomical instrument is being manipulated, probably the cosmograph, models of which have been discovered in Han dynasty tombs. The specific meaning of *kan* is "canopy" and that of *yu* is "chassis," which describes the Chinese chariot, with its boxlike passenger compartment and umbrella-like top. As such, it is a metaphor for the round heaven above the square earth and is thus a kenning for the cosmos. Note that the Xishuipo tomb described above also exhibits this pattern. As regards the cosmograph and related divination boards, *kan* would refer to the rotating circular disc—the male component, and *yu* to the square base plate—the female component (see fig. 20). The divination board is more astrological than geophysical, perhaps, but later accretions would slowly transform it into the familiar *luopan*, or *fengshui* compass, of which it is the precursor (see fig. 14).

Another technique of the *kanyu* system is the art of "charting" the dwelling. In this context, charting refers not to the designing or mapping of a residence but to the River Chart, the esoteric numerical diagram connected to *Zhou Changes* trigram sequences (and indirectly

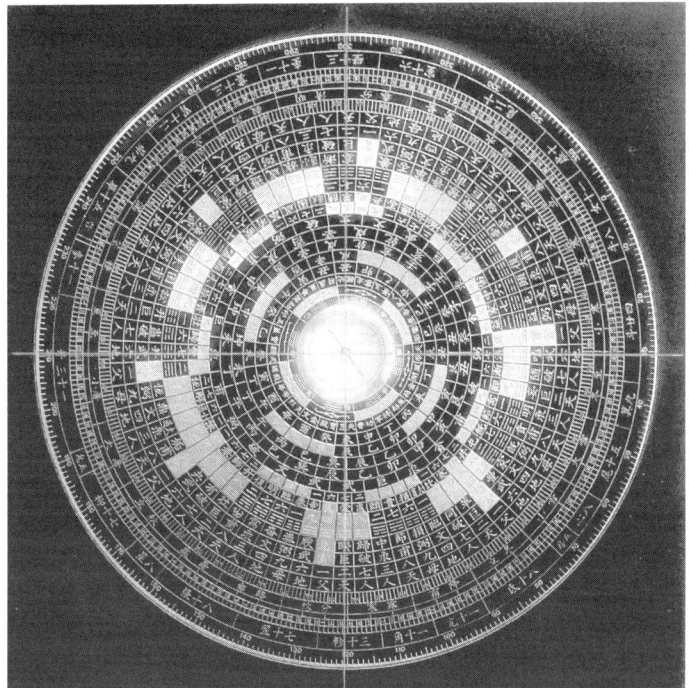

Fig. 14. The Luopan *compass*

to five-phase theories; see pp. 16–17). In its use of the cosmograph and its reliance on five-phase theories to determine auspicious directions, the school of *kanyu* is the ancestor of the Compass School of *fengshui*. Because its methodology originated in trigram numerology, it fits squarely into the *shu,* or numerology, category of divination.

The earliest textual reference to a concept underlying the theories of the Form School of *fengshui* occurs in chapter 39 of *Guanzi,* which dates to no earlier than the fifth century BCE. The passage in question reads: "Water is the blood and breath [*qi*] of the earth, circulating as if in vessels and veins." Not until the Tang dynasty (618–907 CE), in the text of *Book of Burial,* do we see a fully developed theory of the disposition of *qi* in the geophysical plane. The following passage discusses the relationship of form and *qi:* "The *Classic* says: Where the earth takes form, *qi* flows accordingly; thereby things are born.

For *qi* courses within the ground, its flow follows the contour of the ground, and its accumulation results from the halt of terrain." The proper location of the "lair," or burial site, is where the terrain halts, and a large portion of the book describes how to recognize such terrain. Because of its reliance on the observation of topography, this school of *fengshui* conforms to my augury category, or divination by portentous signs (*xiang*).

If the *Book of Burial* may be considered the progenitor of Form School *fengshui*, then the *Yellow Emperor's Dwelling Classic*, also from the Tang dynasty, is the earliest text outlining theories of the Compass School. This book begins by deriding another contemporary practice called the "five surnames" system (which juxtaposed the five-phase value of a person's surname to the five-phase value of the direction faced by the front door of the dwelling). Then it proceeds to illustrate the methodology, using the twenty-four directions, the eight trigrams, and the palace of nine halls to determine auspices.

The real consolidation of *fengshui* theories, if extant texts are any indication, occurred under the tutelage of Yang Yunsong of the Tang dynasty. Yang popularized a Jiangxi method of *fengshui*, named after the district where he supposedly practiced in his later years. Several works attributed to him survive, the most important of which is the *Classic on Rousing the Dragon*, which introduces the nine "stellar" topographic shapes (see p. 78 below). Yang is recognized as the patriarch of the Form School. In the Song dynasty (960–1279 CE), the metaphysical speculations of such scholars as Zhu Xi greatly influenced the development of *fengshui*, which began to place greater emphasis on the trigrams of the *Zhou Changes*. The Compass School gained currency at this time due mainly to the work of the recognized father of Compass School *fengshui*, Lai Wenjun. Another member of this school, Wang Zhaoqing, popularized the use of the *luopan* compass. Since Lai served as an official in Fujian Province, and Wang spent the latter part of his life here, the province gave its name to the method that survived them.

In the following discussion I will analyze in detail both Form School and Compass School *fengshui*. With the former, we are fortunate to have the *Book of Burial*, the first comprehensive treatment of the subject of *fengshui*. This text frequently quotes the lost *Classic of Burial,* attributed to Qingwuzi, a master of "examining earth patterns," whose name first appears in the Han dynasty. However, the book that is attributed to him is probably no earlier than the Three Kingdoms period (220–265 CE). Hence, the practices outlined in the text possibly originate in the early centuries of the common era. With Compass School *fengshui,* we are fortunate to have Qin dynasty daybooks, which collect several different short *fengshui* texts on such subjects as house orientations, gate directions, and building prohibitions. This is the earliest evidence we have of good or bad fortune systematically being connected to direction. After a brief look at this material, I proceed to a detailed analysis of Eight-House *fengshui,* the most popular form of Compass School *fengshui* practiced in the West.

Form School Fengshui

While much has been written on the physiological characteristics of *qi,* on the one hand, and its philosophical and cosmological ramifications, on the other, very little study has been conducted on the concept of *qi* as understood by practitioners of *fengshui.* The premise underlying the theories of *fengshui* is the concept of conglomeration and dispersal. As the reader learned in chapter 1, in the fifth century BCE, Prince Jin first expounded the theory of accumulation and dispersal when trying to dissuade his father from damming the rivers. Whereas the prince was concerned with the geophysical nature of *qi,* the followers of the philosopher Zhuangzi discussed its physiological aspects when they defined birth as the "assembling" of *qi* and death its dispersal.

The physiological *qi* of the Daoists and the geophysical *qi* of Prince Jin merge in the *Book of Burial.* From the opening chapters of this book comes the following passage: "Truly, life is accumulated *qi.* It solidifies into bone, which alone remains after death. Burial returns *qi* to the bones, which is the way the living are endowed." The corpse is interred to receive the influence of the "blood and *qi*" of the body of the earth. Indeed, the metaphor of the earth as *ti* "body" appears directly in the *Book of Burial:* "Earth is the body of *qi*—where there is earth there is *qi. Qi* is the mother of water—where there is *qi* there is water." So the *Book of Burial* also maintains the correspondence between water and *qi* that appears in the *Guanzi* and Prince Jin passages (see pp. 8–10), except that the relationship is clarified in a very important way—*qi* gives birth to water. The relationship is an important one. As mother and offspring, *qi* and water exhibit a natural attraction. Obtaining one is the means of acquiring the other. This is the sine qua non for the practice of *fengshui* and is explained in this passage from the *Book of Burial*, the locus classicus for the term: "The *Classic* says: *Qi* rides the wind [*feng*] and scatters, but is retained when encountering water [*shui*]. The ancients collected it to prevent its dissipation, and guided it to assure its retention. Thus it was called *fengshui*. According to the laws of *fengshui*, the site that attracts water is optimum, followed by the site that catches wind." However, the means by which wind can be collected and water can be guided depends entirely on the topography of the land.

The following passage from the *Book of Burial* describes the relationship between topography, *qi*, and water: "The *Classic* says: Where the ground holds auspicious *qi*, the earth conforms and rises. When *zhi* ridges hold accumulated *qi*, water conforms and accompanies them." Thus, the elevation of features above the level ground is the result of the presence underground of "auspicious *qi*." These topographical features are called *zhi*, a term also borrowed from human physiology, which means arterial branches. Such arteries are the conduits of *qi*, and when they are full of accumulated *qi*, water appears and follows their outward manifestations, the arterial ridges. Since *qi* is the mother of water, presumably the presence of *qi* will generate water. But how does *qi* accumulate in these arteries? Another passage clarifies: "The *Classic* says: Where the earth takes shape, *qi* flows accordingly; thereby things are born. For *qi* courses within the ground, its flow follows the contour of the ground, and its accumulation results from the halt of terrain. For burial, seek the source and ride it to its terminus." The words "contour" and "terrain" translate the same Chinese term, *shi*, a word that in most contexts means "power" or "force." However, at least since the late Warring States period, in combination with the character *xing* (form), it has referred to the inherent strengths of topographical features. Where these features run their course and come to an end is where the *qi* naturally accumulates. According to the *Book of Burial*, "*Qi* collects where forms terminate; it transforms and gives birth to the myriad things. This is exalted ground." Burial should take place in this exalted ground. It would not be an exaggeration to say that in the *Book of Burial*, form and force are the most important technical terms. The author goes to great lengths to explain their meaning, because the search for accumulated *qi* depends entirely on the ability of the *fengshui* master to perceive the subtleties of the topography. In the following passage, form and force are described in some detail: "Arteries spring from lowland terrain; bones spring from mountain terrain. They wind sinuously from east to west and from south to north. Thousands of feet high is called forces; hundreds of feet high is called forms. Forces advance and finish in forms. This is called integrated *qi*. On the land of integrated *qi*, burial occurs in the terminus." The passage begins with another borrowing from human physiology. What previously were called *zhi* branches are here specified even more clearly as "arteries." This view of the flow of *qi* is an old one. In the Qin dynasty, Meng Tian (d. 210 BCE), the builder of the Great Wall, made the following confession: "I could not make the Great Wall without cutting through the veins of the earth" (*Records of the Grand Historian*, chap. 88). We saw previously that the presence of underground *qi* caused the earth to protrude, and here those protrusions are clearly the bulging arteries of the skin of the earth. Bones, on the other hand, rise like ribs high above the earth as mountain ranges. Specifically, as we saw, terrain thousands of feet high is called forces, and terrain only hundreds of feet high is called forms. From a *fengshui* point of view, terrain originates in the forces of alpine heights, slowly winds around as it decreases in altitude, and finally runs its course and finishes in the hills and knolls of the lowlands. When such a terrain can be traced from its highland origin to its lowland terminus, this is the optimum topography. Again, according to the *Book of Burial*, "When the forces are fluid and the forms are dynamic, unwinding from terminus to source, according to the art of *fengshui*, if interment occurs here, good fortune is eternal and misfortune nil."

At this early stage in the development of a methodology to analyze the topography, a technical vocabulary for distinguishing auspicious and inauspicious terrain is still somewhat primitive. Instead, the author of the *Book of Burial* resorts to metaphorical language: "The *Classic* says: Where forces cease and forms soar high, with a stream in front and a hill behind, here hides the head of the dragon. The snout and forehead are auspicious; the horns and eyes bring doom. The ears obtain princes and kings; the lips lead to death or injury from weapons. Where terrain winds about and collects at the center, this is called the belly of the dragon. Where the navel is deep and winding, descendants will have good fortune. If the chest and ribs are injured, burial in the morning will bring sobbing that night." Here we see a picture of the terminus of forces, as if the winding terrain were a coiled dragon. At the point where the mountain range runs its course, terminating in soaring foothills, if the image of a dragon's head can be visualized, this is the ideal locale for burial. This is called the dragon's lair.

If the topography of a particular locale conforms to the descriptions outlined above, then *qi* will be generated along the flow of terrain, and the appearance of water at the terminus will be proof of the coalescence of that *qi*. Thus, a stream flows in front of the dragon's head. This water is the means by which the *qi* generated by the dragon can be harnessed to revive the spirit of the interred bones. According to the *Book of Burial*, "External *qi* is that by which internal *qi* is collected. Water flowing cross-wise is the means for retaining advancing dragons. Lofty forces wind around and come to a rest. If the external has no means to accumulate the internal, *qi* dissipates within the ground. The *Classic* says: The lair that does not hoard will only harbor rotting bones." The water that fronts the burial site must flow transversely across the axis of the advancing mountains. The *Book of Burial* is quite specific in regard to the disposition of this water: "Where water is the Vermilion Bird, decline and prosperity rely on the features of the terrain. Swift currents are taboo and are said to bring grief and lamentation. From a source in the Vermilion Bird, vital *qi* will spring. Waters that diverge will not bring prosperity; pooling waters will accumulate great abundance; stagnant water brings decline. . . . The *Classic* says: Where mountains advance and waters encircle, there is nobility, longevity and wealth. Where mountains imprison and waters flow straight, the king is enslaved and the prince is destroyed." Several important points are made here: (1)

swift currents do not allow the accumulation of *qi*, (2) streams that diverge into tributaries will dissipate collected *qi*, (3) waters that pool naturally in the vicinity of the lair will accumulate *qi*, and (4) from stagnant water comes decline. Thus, springs are auspicious, and the stream thus formed should meander and encircle the lair, pooling its accumulated *qi*. Swift-flowing streams and diverging waters dissipate *qi*, and swamps trap *qi*, thus hindering its natural flow. The Vermilion Bird is one of the "four forces," the other three being the Cerulean Dragon, the White Tiger and the Dark Warrior (or Turtle). These originally referred to the four celestial deities, the four great macro-constellations of the twenty-eight houses of the Chinese zodiac. Here they mark the cardinal directions—the Cerulean Dragon of the east, the Vermilion Bird of the south, the White Tiger of the west, and the Dark Warrior of the north. The ideal lair faces south, the direction of the Vermilion Bird.

Preferably, topographical features should surround the lair. This is to insure that the vital *qi* thus accumulated does not dissipate in the wind: "Blowing *qi* has the ability to dissipate vital *qi*. The dragon and tiger are what protect the district of the lair. On a hill among folds of strata, if open to the left or vacant to the right, if empty in the front or hollow at the rear, vital *qi* will dissipate in the blowing wind. The *Classic* says: A lair with leakage will only harbor a decaying coffin." In practice, however, the features that front the lair to the south should be minimal so that the encircling waters will have means of egress. Those to the east, in the direction of the dragon, should be the most imposing. The features towards the rear of the lair form a backdrop, and the image from the text is of a tomb "backing up to an ornamental screen."

Let us now review the main principles that have been discussed so far and generate a picture of the ideal location of the tomb. First of all, for burial to return *qi* to the bones of the deceased, the ground must lie in the vicinity of accumulated *qi*. To locate accumulated *qi*, one must look for a landscape of integrated *qi*. Such terrain should be continuous from its highest reaches to its terminus, without any breaks in its progression. The vista should be undulating, like the rise and fall of a dragon, and each successive level should decrease in height from its successor. The sequence of features should describe circular contours like a coiling dragon, rather than be angular. Where such terrain runs its course is where *qi* naturally accumulates.

Once accumulated *qi* is located, the lair can be selected. The most auspicious ground will be surrounded by rising terrain. On the east the terrain towers highest and should resemble a recumbent dragon. Opposite this principal feature, toward the west, is another high feature, which should resemble a crouching tiger. Behind the lair toward the north is a topographical form, which backs up to the burial site like an ornamental screen. The terrain toward the south is lowest in elevation. In this direction there should be flowing water, since *qi* is the mother of water. The water should meander, embrace the site, and form pools in front of the lair.

Therefore, a landscape of integrated *qi* will insure that the natural flow of the topographical forces will funnel the *qi* and concentrate it in a single location. The presence of appropriate forms will insure that the wind does not encounter the concentrated *qi* and cause it to dissipate. Since *qi* is the mother of water, the appearance of water in the vicinity of the lair with the proper flow and configuration is proof that *qi* has accumulated beneath the site. If *qi* is present, then the bones of the deceased—the solidified remains of life—will be immersed within that *qi*. The *Zhuangzi* explained how the dispersal of *qi* brings death to the human body. But by the time of Wang Chong (27–97 CE), the Later Han dynasty skeptic, the concept had evolved somewhat: "As water turns into ice, so *qi* crystallizes to form the human body." Furthermore, "That by which man is born is the *qi* of *yin* and *yang*. The *yin qi* produces his bones and flesh; the *yang qi* his vital spirit" (*Discourses Weighed in the Balance*, chap. 62). From Wang Chong's elaboration we can deduce that the *qi* of bones is *yin qi*. So if interred bones are to be charged like a dead battery by the influence of the accumulated *qi* of the burial lair, it must be *yang qi* that has coalesced. The *Book of Burial* identifies accumulated *qi* in several places as "vital" or "living" *qi*. The earliest reference to vital *qi* is in the *Annals of Lu Büwei* in a passage describing the cycle of the seasons. In the last month of spring, we are told, "Vital *qi* flourishes, and *yang qi* flows forth; shoots emerge, and buds unfold" (3/1.3). Vital *qi* is therefore the precursor of *yang qi*, and it is *yang qi* that can energize the bones of the dead.

The process whereby the bones are energized is called "mutual resonance." According to the *Huainanzi*, "Everything is the same as its *qi*; all things respond to their own class" (4.8), and "Things within the same class move each other; root and branch respond to each other" (3.2). The standard proof of mutual resonance given by the ancient philosophers is this: If a string on one lute is plucked, the same string on a nearby lute will simultaneously vibrate. Because the *qi* of the interred corpse and the *qi* of the living descendants are identical, when the vital, life-giving *qi* of the burial site surrounds the bones, they are energized, and the lives of the descendants are thereby endowed.

Compass School Fengshui

The earliest evidence of the actual practice of *fengshui* by the common people is in daybooks discovered in the 1970s in a Qin-era tomb at Shuihudi in Hubei Province. Unlike the content of the *Book of Burial*, the daybook texts, besides describing the homes of the living rather than the tombs of the dead, are largely concerned with directional placement of residences and never once mention the *qi* of a location. As such, these passages are the earliest documentation of the use of directions and positions theories of *fengshui*. In an untitled passage, we are given very specific advice regarding the dimensions of a house and its location in the residential compound. The proximity of the house in relation to livestock pens, grain bins, ponds, roads, and water drains can influence the fortune of the family living in the house. In this section, direction and accompanying auspice are often presented in a context that juxtaposes opposite directions and contrasting auspices.

1. Inner versus outer
   A residence that is low in the middle and higher on all four sides will bring wealth. One that is tall in the middle and lower on all four sides will bring poverty.
2. The cardinal directions
   A residence that is high in the north and low in the south will have no favor. A residence that is high in the south and low in the north is useful to the market. In a residence that is high in the east and low in the west the women will take charge. . . . When the water drain exits to the west there will be poverty and

women will gossip. When the water drain exits to the north, the family will not store wealth. When the water drain exits to the south, the family will benefit. . . . Where the wall is taller in the east than the wall in the west, the gentleman will not obtain loyalty. . . . Place the door in the north or south wall of the residence for good fortune.
3. Right versus left
A residence that is long on the right and short on the left is auspicious. In a residence that is long on the left the women will take charge. . . . Entering the village gate on the right is unlucky.
4. The four corners
It is not advantageous when the granary is located in the northwest corner of the yard. When the granary is located in the southeast corner of the yard, the house is incomplete and gains no advantage. A granary located in the southwest is auspicious. A granary located in the northeast is lucky. . . . A well between a door and window will bring wealth. When the well is located in the southwest corner of the yard, if the husband does not get sick he will become impoverished. If the well is located in the northwest corner, descendants will be cut off.

It is unclear what system is being used to determine auspice in these passages. The lack of a comprehensive body of information concerning the origin and function of these divinatory statements makes it difficult to know what engine, if any, runs the actual and conceptual machinery of this process.

The Eight-House System

One of the most popular forms of residential *fengshui* practiced in the world today is the Eight-House system, also called Nine-Star *fengshui* for reasons that will soon become evident. This branch of *fengshui* can be traced to the Daoist monk, Ruo Guan, of the Qing dynasty (1644–1912), who was the first to write down the principles of the school in his book, *Illuminating the Eight Houses*. Its technique has been called the "MacDonald's" of *fengshui* because of its ease of application—anyone with a compass and a calendar can conduct a *fengshui* reading like an expert. Yet it has also been called the most obscure and difficult to understand of all techniques of *fengshui* because none of the popular texts published since the Qing dynasty adequately explained how the system supposedly works. Because of its immense popularity and apparent simplicity, I will give a detailed explanation of the methodology for conducting readings with Eight-House *fengshui*.

The correlation of the Luo Writing numbers and eight trigrams is the minimum requirement for conducting Eight-House *fengshui* readings (see p. 17). A formula called the great roving year is the means by which number and trigram merge. The roving year is better understood as the roving *star* year, or the year corresponding to the roving Luo number, which may be thought of as a guardian star (see below). First, the sequence of digits one through nine is repeated twenty times to match three sixty-term stem-branch periods of 180 years called the tri-epoch.* Since every year has a stem-branch designation, in the tri-epoch everyone's year of birth has a digital correlate from 1 to 9. Each Luo number has a unique trigram, derived from its post-heaven correlation (see fig. 9), so when the tri-epoch digit is equated with the Luo number, each person has a trigram that corresponds to his or her natal year. This is called the natal trigram, and it identifies the character of cosmic *qi* present at the person's birth. Table 9 shows the guardian star and natal trigram for men and women born between the 1984 and 1992.

Finally, the natal trigram is paired with each of the eight directional trigrams in the post-heaven sequence (called hall or house trigrams). Incidentally, the fifth star—in the center of the Luo Writing—has no direction. Since it shares centrality with earth in the five-phase scheme of the cosmos, it thus corresponds to the mountain trigram (for men) and the earth trigram (for women) both of which share the

---

*A cycle is twenty years. An epoch is three cycles, or sixty years, each designated by a stem-branch pillar. A tri-epoch is therefore 180 years. The three sixty-term periods in the tri-epoch of 180 years are designated the upper, middle, and lower epochs, respectively. The current tri-epoch began in the year 1864 and will terminate in the year 2043. The year 2008, a *wuzi* (5A) pillar, is the twenty-fifth year of the third, or lower, epoch, in the eighth cycle of the great roving year. 2008 is also the 145th year of the current great year.

TABLE 9. GUARDIAN STARS FOR BIRTH YEARS 1984–1992

Male birth year	Female birth year	Guardian Star	Natal Trigram	Phase
1990	1986	1	Water	Water
1991	1985	9	Fire	Fire
1992	1984	8	Mountain	Earth
1984	1992	7	Lake	Metal
1985	1991	6	Heaven	Metal
1986	1990	5	Mountain (m)/ Earth (f)	Earth
1987	1989	4	Wood	Wood
1988	1988	3	Thunder	Wood
1989	1987	2	Earth	Earth

earth phase. So there are eight natal trigrams for the nine guardian stars, and each natal trigram has eight corresponding hall trigrams. This complement of a natal trigram and its set of hall trigrams represents a metaphysical interaction between the individual's natal *qi* and the *qi* of the environment that surrounds that individual. This conjunction is essentially thought of as a transformation of the natal trigram into the hall trigram and vice versa, and each transformation is capable of generating good or bad fortune for the individual. The auspice generated by the conjunction is known as the Nine Stars.

The provenance of the concept of Nine Stars is unknown, but the scant textual evidence suggests that it was religious in origin. The unusual nouns (see table 10) name the seven stars of the Big Dipper, plus two secret "companions" to the penultimate star of the handle. There is a considerable body of legend attached to these stars, which were recognized as deities by fourth-century Daoist priests. By the late Tang dynasty, when *fengshui* texts such as the *Classic on Rousing the Dragon* were written, the Nine Stars referred to archetypal terrestrial counterparts of the celestial namesakes, mountain shapes that seemingly have nothing to do with the original star names. In this function, the stars referred to isolated mountain peaks surrounding the dragon lair and were thus classifications of Form School *fengshui*.

Fengshui, or Tomb and Residential Site Orientation

Finally, by the time Eight-House *fengshui* flourished in the Qing dynasty, the Nine Stars were names for the eight levels of auspice associated with trigram transformation. Due at least to their celestial origin, but also owing to their status as numerological forces of nature, the Nine Stars are considered to be good and evil spirits conferring good fortune or misfortune on the individual.

Let us now return to the roving star year. When the natal trigram is known, it is compared with each of the eight directional hall trigrams. The divergence of lines across the space of each pair of trigrams determines the star that will govern a particular direction for that particular person. Each star in turn is characterized by a specific auspice. For example, if the natal trigram and the hall trigram differ by only the top line, the Ravenous Wolf star governs the transformation, and the auspice is great fortune. Table 10 enumerates the four lucky stars and the four unlucky stars, their unique auspices, and the diverging lines that mark the transformation from one trigram to the next. Note that the Nine Stars are ranked in the table from most to least auspicious. In practice, the two companion stars are subsumed

TABLE 10. NINE-STAR AUSPICE

The Nine Stars	Auspice	Diverging Lines
Ravenous Wolf	Life Breath / Great Fortune	Top Line
The Warrior	Extended Years / Great Fortune	All Lines Diverge
Great Gate	Celestial Doctor / Lesser Fortune	Middle Line / Bottom Line
Left, Right Guardian	Neutral / Small Fortune	No Lines Diverge
Stored Blessings	Accident & Injury / Lesser Misfortune	Bottom Line
The Scholar	Six Curses / Lesser Misfortune	Top Line / Bottom Line
Virtue	Five Ghosts / Great Misfortune	Middle Line / Top Line
Conquered Army	Shortened Life / Great Misfortune	Middle Line

TABLE 11. THE HOUSE OF QIAN

Natal Trigram	Hall Trigram	Direction	Nine Star Auspice
☰ Qian	☱ Dui	West	Ravenous Wolf, Life Breath, Great Fortune
☰ Qian	☷ Kun	Southwest	The Warrior, Extended Years, Great Fortune
☰ Qian	☶ Gen	Northeast	Great Gate, Celestial Doctor, Lesser Fortune
☰ Qian	☰ Qian	Northwest	Guardians, Neutral, Small Fortune
☰ Qian	☲ Li	South	Conquered Army, Shortened Life, Great Misfortune
☰ Qian	☳ Zhen	East	Virtue, Five Ghosts, Great Misfortune
☰ Qian	☵ Kan	North	The Scholar, Six Curses, Lesser Misfortune
☰ Qian	☴ Xun	Southeast	Stored Blessings, Accident & Injury, Lesser Misfortune

into one and represent the situation where the natal trigram and the hall trigram are the same. This direction is usually reserved for the front door of the residence.

To provide an example of a great roving year transformation, table 11 uses the trigram *qian* as the natal trigram and then lists the eight hall trigrams, their directions, and the accompanying auspices from table 10. From tables 10 and 11 it can be seen that of the eight directional auspices for each natal trigram of the Nine-Star system, four are auspicious and four are inauspicious.

If the remaining natal trigrams are expanded according to the great roving year transformations as in table 11, an interesting phenomenon emerges. Half of the natal trigrams are fortunate matches with the same four hall trigrams—specifically, the directions west, southwest, northeast, and northwest, as in table 11. And the other half of the natal trigrams are fortunate matches with the remaining four hall trigrams—specifically, the directions south, east, north, and southeast. These two groups of trigrams are called the four eastern

Fengshui, or Tomb and Residential Site Orientation 81

halls and the four western halls and form the configuration shown in figure 15 around the post-heaven sequence of trigrams. If the birthdate is known, the four lucky halls and the four unlucky halls can be easily derived, and the individual will then know which is the most appropriate direction in which to face the house or orient its rooms. In general, the front door and living areas of the home should occupy fortunate directions; storage rooms, bathrooms, and unoccupied rooms should be located in sectors identified with misfortune.

Most of the popular texts that discuss the Eight-House methodology rely on five-phase correlations to explain the derivation of auspices. The supposition of popular *fengshui* methodology is that when the five-phase value of the natal trigram is matched with the five-phase value of the directional trigram, good fortune is indicated when the two exhibit a relationship of mutual production, whereas bad fortune is indicated when the two exhibit a relationship of mutual conquest. For example, let us imagine that a person with the natal trigram *xun* wanted to build a house facing north. From figure 16, we see that *xun* is in the wood phase, whereas the direction north is occupied by the trigram *kan,* which is in the water phase. In the mutual production order of the five phases, water nourishes wood, so this conjunction of *xun* and *kan* would indicate good fortune. From table 11 we see that the *xun* and *kan* trigrams differ by the top line, and table 10 confirms that the Ravenous Wolf star, which brings great fortune, governs this transformation. Conversely, suppose the

Eastern Hall XUN	Eastern Hall LI	Western Hall KUN
Eastern Hall ZHEN		Western Hall DUI
Western Hall GEN	Eastern Hall KAN	Western Hall QIAN

Fig. 15. Eastern and western halls

same person wanted to build a house facing southwest. The direction southwest is occupied by the trigram *kun,* which is in the earth phase. In the mutual conquest order of the five phases, wood saps earth, so the conjunction of *xun* and *kun* would indicate bad fortune. From table 11 we see that the *xun* and *kun* trigrams differ by the middle and top lines, and table 10 confirms that this transformation is governed by the star Virtue, which brings great misfortune. In similar fashion, five-phase theory can predict the auspice of the remaining six directions of the natal trigram *xun.* Figure 17 compiles all the information outlined above for the House of Xun, whose occupant was born when the wood phase was dominant. It also suggests appropriate room designations for the eight halls of the house, based on the relative auspice of each direction.

In this fashion, the interaction of two sequences of mystical symbols — the post-heaven trigrams and the Luo Writing numbers — is able to describe a mantic significance for the relationship between individual humans and their specific environments. From the point of view of the *fengshui* client, the transformation of one symbol into another conjures up a star spirit, which visits good or bad fortune upon the person who by chance or choice resides in that space at that time. Those who wish to seek the good or avoid the bad can employ the theories of five-phase orders to predict the fortune of their anthropocosmic conjunction. Although no one can seriously argue that this numerical foundation is a claim for a scientific basis of *fengshui*

XUN Wood SE	LI Fire South	KUN Earth SW
ZHEN Wood East		DUI Metal West
GEN Earth NE	KAN Water North	QIAN Metal NW

Fig. 16. Eight-House trigrams with five-phase correlations

SE Wood Wood joins Wood Small Fortune FRONT DOOR	S Fire Wood feeds Fire Great Fortune LIVING ROOM	SW Earth Wood saps Earth Great Misfortune BATHROOM
E Wood Wood joins Wood Great Fortune DINING ROOM	**HOUSE OF XUN**	W Metal Metal cuts Wood Lesser Misfortune KITCHEN
NE Earth Wood saps Earth Great Misfortune STORAGE	N Water Water nurtures Wood Great Fortune MASTER BEDROOM	NW Metal Metal cuts Wood Lesser Misfortune GUEST BEDROOM

Fig. 17. The House of Xun

theories, at the same time it is good evidence that this method of divination is neither arbitrary nor capricious. As with most forms of divination discussed in this book, the existence of a key transforms what appears on the surface to be an irrational art or an unfathomable mystery into a rational and reasonable system of thought. In ancient China such reasoned divination methodologies took their place alongside other rational practices such as medicine and government administration. For that reason alone they are worthy of the scholar's study and the public's respect.

CHAPTER 5

Numerology, or Divination by Counting

I have borrowed the term "numerology" to name divination by numbers or counting. In the Chinese tradition, there are a dizzying variety of numerical methods used to divine the future. The reader has seen a detailed analysis of milfoil stalk-counting, but there are also *Yi*-style divination techniques using coins. Other objects, such as bamboo sticks and ivory chessmen, are also used for counting. And there are numerical calculations based on such things as the time of birth or the time of divination. In this chapter, I mention only the most prominent, either because of their importance in the development of Chinese divination or because of their contemporary popularity. I begin with a look at divination systems based on the manipulation of milfoil stalks.

Milfoil Divination

Milfoil divination includes those systems using the manuals discussed in chapters 2 and 3, in addition to a newly discovered system referred to as numerical hexagrams, which will begin the discussion below. Because previous chapters have discussed the *Zhou Changes* and *Guicang* in great detail, I will not repeat that information here. However, there is one more well-known book of divination that originated in the classical period, the Han dynasty *Taixuanjing*, or *Canon of the Great Mystery*, which was also consulted through the medium of milfoil. Eventually, because the manipulation of milfoil stalks was so complicated, the Chinese developed other counting systems for use with *Yi*-style manuals. I will discuss some of those streamlined systems here.

1. Numerical hexagrams

    The so-called numerical hexagrams were first recognized in the Northern Song dynasty (960–1127) but were considered

Numerology, or Divination by Counting

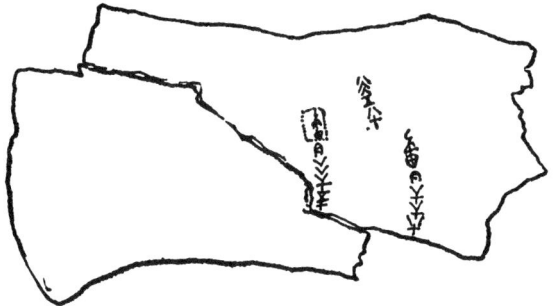

*Fig. 18. Shang dynasty numerical hexagrams
(after* Kaogu *1989, no. 7, p. 638)*

"strange words" and were not known to be numbers until the twentieth century (see fig. 18). So far, over a hundred of these numerical hexagrams have been discovered on Shang and Zhou oracle bones, Zhou dynasty bronzes, Warring States–era bamboo slips, and Qin and Han pottery jars. While the specific divinatory procedure is unclear, it is likely to be another form of *Yi*-style divination. Scholars explain the phenomenon of numerical hexagrams as follows.

When all the existing records of numerical hexagrams are compared, it turns out that the six-digit numbers consist only of the numerals 1, 5, 6, 7, and 8. Since the ancient Chinese numerals for 1 through 4 are sets of one to four horizontal lines, apparently the numerals 2, 3, and 4 do not occur in records because they are too difficult to distinguish if they appear in succession in a vertical stack. What looks like a 4 (a stack of four horizontal lines) might actually be a 1 and a 3 or two 2's. From a statistical analysis of the record, it was determined that the numerals 2 and 4 were transmuted into 6, and the numeral 3 was transmuted into 1. Theoretically, as the record evolved, the numerals 5, 7, and 8 also disappeared, leaving six-term sequences of only the numerals 1 and 6. The example in the center of the Shang bone in figure 18—866587—would now have been represented as 666161. In other words, the numeral 1 subsumed all odd digits, and the numeral 6 subsumed all

Fig. 19. Qin dynasty hexagram

even digits. This example would then have appeared as the illustration in figure 19. The numeral 1, then, as now, was a simple horizontal stroke. The numeral 6 was a wedge or caret. This numerical symbol of lines and wedges is precisely how the hexagrams appear in the Wangjiatai bamboo slip manuscript of the *Guicang*.

2. Great Mystery divination

The *Canon of the Great Mystery* was created in the Western Han dynasty by Yang Xiong (53 BCE–18 CE), based on the *Zhou Changes*. Where the *Changes* has two different lines (*yin* and *yang*), the *Great Mystery* has three different lines—unbroken (representing heaven), broken once (representing earth), and broken twice (representing man). The *Great Mystery*'s method of casting milfoil stalks to obtain numbers is similar to that of the *Changes,* except that the diviner begins with thirty-six stalks instead of forty-nine. Whereas the six-line hexagram of the *Changes* has six positions progressing from the bottom upward, the *Great Mystery*'s tetragram has four lines progressing from the top downward. The four positions are demarcated as follows: regions, provinces, departments, and families. Each tetragram is accompanied by a head text and nine appraisal texts, which are not tied to the tetragram's lines like the hexagram and line statements of the *Changes*. Instead, the appraisals are linked to (1) cosmic cycles (the year, *yin* and *yang*, and the five phases), (2) the divination situation (time of day, stages of action and response), and (3) social hierarchy (common man, ministers, ruler). All such correlations interact in the divination event. Auspice is then determined when the *yin* and *yang* quality of the three types of appraisal are the same or different as the *yin* and *yang* quality of the head text.

The following description of the *Great Mystery* structure is by Nathan Sivin, who believes that the book "is superior to the *Classic of Changes* for many of the uses to which Europeans have long put the latter."

> The single Supreme Mystery stands for the cosmos as a whole. It occupies the center of the universe and the political realm, as the emperor does, where the three regions of heaven, man, and earth come together. Each of the three regions is divided into three provinces, to correspond to the ideal nine of the Han empire, and each of those into three departments, corresponding to the Han sub-provincial level. The ultimate eighty-one families stand for the multiplicity of individual phenomena in society and Nature. Each tetragram is associated with a "Head text" (*shou*) set out in three parts, a title, an image that refers to yin–yang, and an image related to the "myriad phenomena" or "all things" (*wanwu*) of the natural order. The title of the tetragram, a single graph, names one aspect of the comprehensive Mystery, such as "Measure" (*du*, Head 52), and "Eternal" (*yong*, Head 53), to which humans respond for good or ill. The next line describes in poetic language the evolution of yang or yin *qi* during that precise phase in the annual cycle. The remainder of each text describes the effect of that evolution upon the phenomena of Nature.*

Due to the difficulty of its methodology, the *Great Mystery* is rarely used in modern China, even though the language of its lines is quite straightforward. According to Sivin, it was the poetic language and philosophical vigor of the *Great Mystery* that insured its transmission throughout the ages, not its use in divination practice.

---

*Nathan Sivin, *Medicine, Philosophy and Religion in Ancient China* (Aldershot, UK: Variorum, 1995), ch. 3, p. 20.

3. Plum Blossom and similar methods of counting
As milfoil divination spread from the court to the marketplace, its methodology necessarily changed because its numerological complexity was too difficult or too time-consuming for the common consumer. Thus, over the centuries, folk practitioners developed a series of simple and convenient procedures for obtaining hexagrams. Here I will introduce some of the most common.

Plum Blossom Counting. First, based on the earth branch for the year, day, and month, determine the decimal number for each branch based on its position in the twelve-term series. Add these numbers together and divide by 8 (for the eight trigrams); the remainder, a number between 1 and 8, determines the top trigram of the hexagram (numerical values here are based on the so-called Fuxi order of trigrams—derived from the pre-heaven sequence; see figs. 4 and 6). Then determine the branch for the double-hour of the day and add its number to the figure for the year, month, and day. Divide this number by 8 to determine the bottom trigram. Finally, divide the same number by 6 (for the number of lines in a hexagram); the remainder, a number between 1 and 6, determines the changing line. Plum blossom numerology was transmitted by Shao Yong (1011–1077), who supposedly conceived of this form of divination while viewing flowers in a garden.

Washing for Gold. Select two Chinese characters and count the number of strokes in each. Using the pre-heaven sequence of trigrams, count off by the number of strokes in the first character to determine the upper trigram and by the number of strokes in the second character to determine the lower trigram. Then count off by sixes the total number of strokes in both characters; the remainder will be the changing line. The characters used for this type of divination might be the name of a city one is planning to visit, or the name of a person or business, and so on.

4. Fire Pearl Collection

The Fire Pearl Collection (*Huozhulin*) method of divination now generally refers to any coin-toss method for casting the *Classic of Changes*. As such, it is also known as the Wen Wang method. The coin toss proceeds in this fashion. Using three coins of the same denomination, the diviner tosses them to determine the proper line of the hexagram. Each throw will return one of the following combinations of heads (*yin*, value=2) and tails (*yang*, value=3):

- If all three coins are tails, then it is an old *yang* line (9).
- If all three coins are heads, then it is an old *yin* line (6).
- If one coin is tails and two coins are heads, then it is a young *yang* line (7).
- If one coin is heads, and two coins are tails, then it is a young *yin* line (8).

Six throws of the three coins will result in the complete hexagram.

Fire Pearl Collection is also the name of a text purportedly written by a Buddhist monk in the tenth century. Many of the complicated procedures of this form of divination can be traced back to Jing Fang. As such, its unusual name also betrays an origin in the Daoist alchemical tradition, since the fire pearl is another name for the elixir of immortality. The procedure is as follows. The diviner tosses the coins to determine the proper hexagram and its changing lines. Then he finds the hexagram's location among the Eight Palaces (which also identifies the palace's five-phase correlation), in addition to the hexagram's position in the palace (first through fifth generation, wandering or homing soul). Then he determines (1) the generation line (based on changing lines), which represents the divination subject (self), and (2) the corresponding line in the other trigram, which represents the object (other). Then he "inserts the stems" and determines the five-phase values of each line. Finally, he establishes the social relationship governed by each line. If there are changing lines (forming a new hexagram), the diviner must also insert

TABLE 12. LINE RELATIONSHIPS

Relationship	Five-phase Interaction
Parents and ancestors	The line produces the palace.
Brothers, sisters, and peers	The line equals the palace.
Officials, superiors, and threats	The line conquers the palace.
Descendants	The palace produces the line.
Spouse, wealth, and profession	The palace conquers the line.

the stem and branch times, five-phase values, family members, and so on, for those lines. Table 12 indicates how the five-phase value of the individual line interacts with the value of the palace in order to determine the line's relationship. This is the first stage of the procedure—the spatial observation—which obtains a general forecast based on the content of the hexagram line texts in relation to the character of the individual lines.

Next, the diviner conducts a temporal observation by first ascertaining the hexagram body (also called the hexagram month). He then records the day of the month and determines the six (animal) spirits (dark turtle, white tiger, rising serpent, *gouchen*, red bird, green dragon). The time of divination determines such factors as the functional spirit, the original spirit, the taboo spirit, the entering spirit, the departing spirit, the flying spirit, the hidden spirit, and so on, which reveal themselves in the hexagram. For example, if the functional spirit of the hexagram is metal, then earth is the original spirit (because earth harbors metal ores), fire is the taboo spirit (because fire melts metal), and wood is the enemy spirit (because metal cuts wood); water can conquer the taboo spirit (fire) and can produce the enemy spirit (wood). During an actual divination ceremony, while combining spatial and temporal factors, the diviner must analyze the production and conquest relationships of the five-phase qualities of all factors in order to determine the proper fortune.

Divining by Objects

Besides milfoil-counting numerology, another common practice is to use objects encountered in normal life to obtain numbers for determining auspice.

1. Bamboo Spindle
The Bamboo Spindle form of divination was transmitted from southeastern China. In his poem "Encountering Sorrow," the Warring States–era poet, Qu Yuan, tells the story of how a shaman used Bamboo Spindle to divine for him. The name of this particular divining art refers to the process of knotting grass and breaking bamboo in order to ascertain good and bad fortune. In practice, the diviner grasps a handful of bamboo joints, grass stalks, or twigs, without knowing the number. Then, in the manner of milfoil-stalk manipulation, he counts them out by threes hand by hand. By the number placed between his fingers, he ascertains good and bad fortune.

2. Cups
"Cups" is the name of a divination tool shaped like a clamshell or a crescent moon. These can be made of jade, bamboo, or wood and have one flat and one rounded side. When divining, two cups are thrown on the ground and then observed to see which side is up. Bad fortune is indicated if both cups land flat side or round side down; if one flat side is up and the other down, good fortune is indicated. The Chinese word for cups, *beijiao*, can be written various ways, including using words meaning "horned cups" or "teaching cups." The character *jiao*, regardless of how written, simply refers to this divinatory tool. See chapter 7 for an account of this form of divination in use.

Fate-Calculation

The fundamental theory of fate-calculation holds that one's destiny is related to one's time of birth; furthermore, the recording of this time is determined by the position of the heavenly bodies. Consequently, fate-calculation is usually divided into two systems: the traditional Four Pillars or Eight Characters system that records time of birth, and related systems that use astrological terminology. These latter systems are not horoscopes per se, because they do not depend on the position of actual stars in the sky for their efficacy. All these systems are based on time, and the calculation of time is connected closely with theories of *yin* and *yang*, the five phases, and *Zhou Changes* hexagram lines.

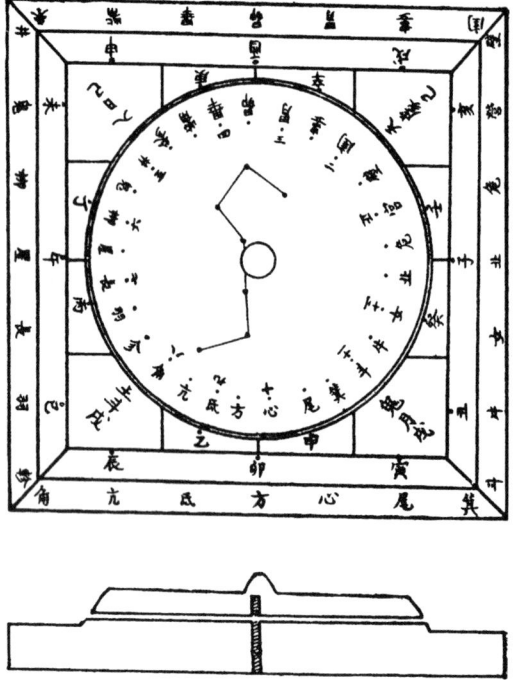

Fig. 20. The Six-Ren board (after Kaogu 1978, no. 5, p. 340)

1. Six-*Ren* divination

    One of the oldest forms of fate-calculation—attestable since the late Warring States period from unearthed divination boards, is the system known as *liuren,* or the Six-*Ren.* As illustrated here (see fig. 20), the board consisted of a round heaven disk on top that rotated on a pivot set into a square earth plate on the bottom. On the outer edge of both the square and round plates are arranged the names of the twenty-eight constellations of the Chinese zodiac. The twelve months are arranged by decimal number counterclockwise inside the ring of the heaven disc, while the twelve earth branches are arranged clockwise on the second row of the earth plate. Eight of the ten heaven stems are inscribed on the innermost square, along with four gates at the corners. In the center of the round disk was inscribed a representation of the constellation Beidou, or the Big Dipper. Other Han dynasty versions of the board have a more complicated heaven dial of up to three rings, adding the earth branches and the Twelve Spirits to the twenty-eight constellations.

The function of this ancient instrument was at least nominally astronomical and was certainly astrological. Although the record is sparse regarding the function of such instruments, the following analysis of its use in astronomical observation will give the reader a better notion of just how the ancient Chinese visualized the heavens. If one observes the southern sky at the same time each night for several nights in succession, the zodiacal constellations will appear to move from east to west in a great arc. The dial of the board as it is rotated clockwise on the earth plate corresponds to the arc made by the stars as they pass toward their setting in the west. Ancient Chinese astronomers were fully aware that the quarterly (six-hour) diurnal rotation of the heavens was equivalent to the seasonal (tri-monthly) annual revolution. With a knowledge of what star was passing the meridian at sunset, one could glance at the board and tell which constellation had culminated at noon or which would be culminating at midnight. By means of the board, the configuration of the heavens could be determined at any time of day or night for any month. Based on this function of the Six-*Ren* board—where it resembles a "cosmic clock"—scholars have dubbed the instrument a "cosmograph."

First, the cosmographer would orient the earth board to the cardinal directions, represented by the four sides of the board. Then he would align the number of the month on the heaven disc with the double-hour of the day or night from the earth plate. Finally he would note the constellations on the portion of the disc that fronted the southern edge of the board. These are the asterisms that would appear in the sky in the month and hour of the query. Or, knowing that a particular constellation had risen at sunset on the vernal equinox, a person would know which constellation was rising, culminating, or setting on the summer solstice. More importantly, perhaps, the disposition of the Dipper's handle could be predicted. Beidou (and the Purple Palace, discussed below) was the throne of Shang Di, the High God, and the handle indicated the focus of his power.

However, manipulating the dial was also a prognostic art that allowed the diviner to predict the future. It is this function of the instrument that gave the form of divination its name. When the ten heaven stems are matched with the twelve earth branches to form the sixty-term sexagesimal cycle (see pp. 18–19), there are a total of six terms that begin with *ren* (stem 9) — thus *liu* (six) *ren*, or "six nines." Six-*Ren* divination is based solely on five-phase theories. The ten stems are paired with the five phases (see table 2), so that each phase governs two stems, one of which is *yang*, and the other *yin*. The *ren* stem has *yang* polarity and belongs to the water phase. When the stems are then matched with particular branches, which also have five-phase correlates (table 3), the interaction produces good or bad fortune based on the rules of five-phase production and conquest.

As we saw above, the heaven disc of the Six-*Ren* board demarcates the twelve months. Conversely, the earth plate is surrounded by the twelve earth branches and the ten heaven stems. In order to conduct a fortune-telling session, the board is used in a similar fashion as that outlined above, except that it is not the motion of constellations that the fortune-teller seeks but the confluence of phases of *qi*. The divination event makes use of two different components — the time of the ceremony and another factor obtained by chance. The diviner first ascertains the time component by locating the number of the current month on the heaven dial. This identifies which of the Twelve Spirits is currently governing the heavens. He then establishes the chance component by asking the enquirer to randomly choose a number between 1 and 12. He then locates this number (by earth branch) on the earth plate. Finally, the heaven dial is rotated so that the number of the month matches the random branch selected on the earth plate. The Six-*Ren* board is fixed in this position, and subsequent readings will be based on this configuration. Next, the random number is located on the heaven disk (rather than on the earth plate) and its corresponding branch on the earth plate is noted. Finally, this branch is sited on the heaven disk. This final point on the heaven disk situates the Twelve Heavenly Generals around the Six-*Ren* board—they name the twelve different auspices determined by the interaction of the five-phase values of the various correlations.

At this point in the divination ceremony, the diviner incorporates the day into his calculations (which has both stem and branch components). In this fashion, he determines which of the generals are involved in the prognostication and what their messages are. While this form of divination seems quite complicated to the uninitiated, it is actually considered quite easy by diviners and can even be conducted without the assistance of the cosmograph. In the famous Ming dynasty (1368–1644) novel, *Romance of the Three Kingdoms*, the great statesman Zhuge Liang often uses the fingers of his hand to conduct Six-*Ren* divination. This technique is called "divining in the sleeve."

2. Six Wands

Liubo, or Six Wands, is another form of fate-calculation with an ancient history. Reputed to have originated in the Shang dynasty, the earliest textual reference to this form of divination is in the third-century BCE poem, "Summoning the Soul":

> With bamboo sticks and ivory men,
> They compete in Six Wands.
> Taking sides and pushing ahead,
> They compel each other forcefully.

Several Six Wands sets have been discovered in Qin and Han dynasty tombs, so we have a detailed picture of the board and its pieces. We also have many clues regarding the function of this type of divination, which took the form of a competition. In this sense, it differs from all other forms of divination discussed in this book. Unfortunately, there is no clear record of how the game was played.

*Fig. 21. Fourth-century BCE Six Wands board
(after* Wenwu *1979, no. 1, p. 26)*

The Six Wands board is reminiscent of the Six-*Ren* board in its square shape and gradated edges. However, the Six Wands gradations are curious designs resembling the letters T, L, and V. The most ornate example of the board is a stone version excavated from a late Warring States–era tomb at Pingshan in Hebei Province (see fig. 21). Scholars speculate that the TLV marks represent roads around which the players moved their chessmen. In 1993 a Han dynasty tomb at Yinwan Village in Jiangsu Province produced several divination texts, including a wooden document with a replica of a Six Wands board accompanied by divinatory formulae. Around the roads of this replica were incised the sixty pairs of stems and branches. How the pieces moved was likely determined by the throw of six bamboo wands, which were found along with the earliest versions of the boards. Eventually the game would be played with dice.

Some of the earliest references to the function of the Six Wands board describe men competing with spirits or immortals in order to gain power or long life. The *Records of the Grand Historian* notes that King Wu Yi of the Shang dynasty (r. 1198–1194 BCE) played Six Wands against a puppet made to represent a heavenly deity. In the *Intrigues of the Warring Kingdoms* is the story of a young man who played Six Wands against a grove spirit, seeking its power. Making throws with his left hand for the spirit and with his right hand for himself, he won the competition. The grove died seven days later.

3. The Four Pillars or Eight Characters

The Four Pillars method of fate-calculation is the most commonly used system in the Chinese-speaking world for determining the ebb and flow of fortune. A person's time of birth was recorded using numbers of the sexagesimal cycle (see pp. 18–19). The sixty stem-branch combinations (or "pillars") were used to designate hours, days, months, and years. Thus, a person's year, month, day, and hour of birth (the four pillars) were represented by four pairs of stems and branches (the eight characters). Using this information to conduct divination was called Four Pillars Eight Character fate-calculation. The system originated with Li Xuzhong in the Tang dynasty, who is said to have used only the year, month, and day to conduct his calculations. Then, in the Song dynasty a famous fortune-teller named Xu Ziping added a fourth pillar for the twelve double-hours of the twenty-four-hour day to develop the Four Pillars system. For this reason it is also called Ziping divination. In modern China some diviners consider Four Pillars not accurate enough for detailed calculation, so they divide one two-hour period into eight fifteen-minute portions and add another pillar to make Five Pillars and therefore Ten Characters.

The basic methodology of Ziping fate-calculation is as follows. First, the eight stem and branch pairs for the year, month, day, and hour of birth of the person having the fortune told are obtained. Then, the "contained note" phase for each stem-branch combination is figured.* Depending on whether the stem or branch is ruled by *yang* or *yin*, the pillars are identified as follows: the *year* stem and branch is used to represent the ancestors (and one's birth); the *month* stem and branch is used to represent the parents (and one's youth); the *day stem* represents the self, while the *day branch* represents the spouse (and one's adult life); the *hour stem* represents the son, and the *hour branch* represents the daughter (and one's old age). The self is the reference point for the other seven relationships; in such manner the stages of the life cycle are mapped to reveal one's strengths and weaknesses. A balance of *yin* and *yang* and a harmony of phases (more generation than conquest) signal strength and good fortune. Disequilibrium means weakness and misfortune.

Other calculations commonly conducted are: the Fate Palace (an earth branch calculation based on the hour of birth related to the month of birth), the Day of Conception (266 days before birth), the Great Destiny (based on a decade of life), the Small Cycle (based on a year of life), and the Coming Year. These are matched with the annual position of Jupiter (which has a twelve-year cycle) and the Monthly Ordinances (a seasonal indicator of social, political, and economic undertakings) in order to divine the rise and fall of the person's fortune. The Four Pillars fate-calculation system spread to every country in East

---

*The *nayin* "contained note," a technical term adopted from music phraseology, is one of the five phases that results from the pairing of the stem and branch for a given year (or month, or day, etc.), so adopted because the five tones of the pentatonic scale were each associated with a phase. Because there are twelve music regulations (six *yang* and six *yin*), each containing five tones, there are sixty notes altogether, represented by the sixty stem-branches. Each of the sixty notes, and therefore each of the sixty stem-branch combinations, belongs to a particular phase. The phase to which a stem-branch belongs is called the contained note of the stem-branch. Moreover, the stems and branches are considered to produce and conquer one another, as the five phases do.

and Southeast Asia and is the most popular form of divination in Asia today.

4. Purple Palace

Ziwei doushu or Purple Palace Ladle Numbers is a form of astral fate-calculation performed by correlating the eight characters of a person's birth time with the so-called Twelve Palaces. The origin of Purple Palace divination is the Han dynasty worship of the stellar deity *Taiyi*, or the Great Unity, the god of the North Star. Great Unity divination reached its height in the Tang dynasty when its diviners calculated the position of the god as he traveled through the nine palaces of the magic square. In this sense, it is similar to Nine-Star divination (see below). However, the number of palaces in Purple Palace divination is twelve rather than the nine of Great Unity, and Ho Peng Yoke has shown evidence that it owes its most telling feature—the Twelve Palaces—to Western astrology (transmitted to China by Nestorian Christians in the Tang dynasty).

The names and qualities of the Twelve Palaces are as follows: the Life Palace foretells one's character and personality; the Parents Palace foretells one's relationship with parents and superiors; the Happiness Palace foretells one's state of contentment and chance of longevity; the Property Palace foretells one's material possessions; the Career Palace foretells one's career and accomplishments; the Friends Palace foretells one's relationships with friends and employees; the Travel Palace foretells one's fortunes away from home, including in the public sphere; the Illness Palace foretells one's state of health; the Wealth Palace foretells one's financial situation; the Children Palace foretells one's relations with descendants; the Marriage Palace foretells one's relationship with one's husband or wife; and the Brothers Palace foretells one's relationships with one's siblings and colleagues.

Each palace represents a particular time in a person's life: either a double hour of the day, a month, a year, or a decade. Furthermore, stars of good or ill fortune are located in each palace and interact with the character of that palace to determine a person's particular fortune for some period. Most of the names of these stars correspond to actual stars in the Chinese sky. The term Purple Palace refers to two constellations forming barriers around the North Star. This double wall is called the Purple Forbidden Enclosure, which is a stellar analogue of the Forbidden City, that is, the earthly imperial palace. Since the Purple Palace is the celestial court, the Chinese also consider it to be a metonym for the celestial emperor. Beidou, the Northern Ladle (or Big Dipper), forms a third wall. A third constellation, Nandou, the Southern Ladle, is also considered to influence people's fortunes. It is the first constellation of the Dark Warrior (or Turtle), the macro-constellation symbolizing north in Chinese cosmology.

Different schools of Purple Palace fate-calculation use different numbers of stars; however, the fourteen major stars are the following, accompanied by their attributes: the Purple Palace (nobleness); the Great *Yang* (love, generosity); the Warrior Star (wealth, courage); the Star of Virtue (wickedness, cunning); the Ravenous Wolf Star (desire, deceit); the Great Gate Star (suspicion, dishonesty); and the Conquered Army Star (calamity, exhaustion), all purportedly composing the Big Dipper constellation; the Treasury Star (talent, mercy); the Great *Yin* (grace, purity); the Minister Star (honesty, helpfulness); the Ridgepole Star (constancy, leadership); the Star of Seven Auspices (obstinacy); the Armillary Star (wisdom, goodness); and the Harmony Star (modesty), all supposedly composing the Southern Dipper constellation.

Readers may recognize five of these stars from my discussion of Nine-Star *fengshui*. Here I have also given their attributes as they function in Purple Palace fate-calculation. The remaining four of the Nine Stars—the Scholar Star, the Stored Blessings Star, and the Left and Right Guardians—are minor stars in the Purple Palace system. As I pointed out in chapter 4, these stars represent trigram transformations. Figure 22 shows an example of a star chart. Each palace is influenced by (1) its adjacent palaces, (2) the opposite palace (six palaces away), and (3) the related harmony palaces (four palaces to either side). Opposite palaces have the strongest influence on each other. When there

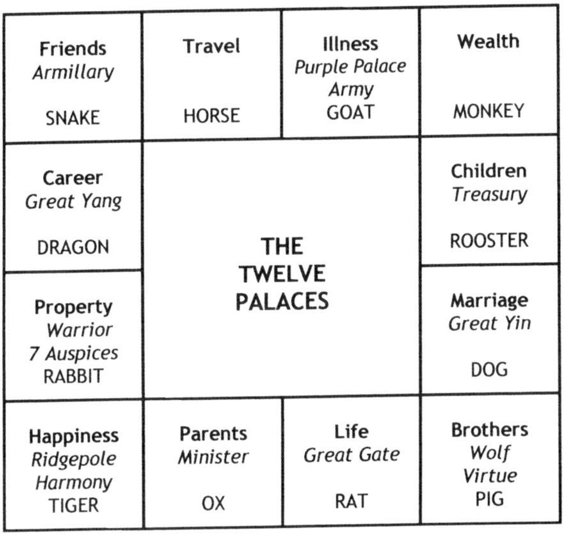

Friends *Armillary* SNAKE	Travel HORSE	Illness *Purple Palace Army* GOAT	Wealth MONKEY
Career *Great Yang* DRAGON	THE TWELVE PALACES		Children *Treasury* ROOSTER
Property *Warrior* *7 Auspices* RABBIT			Marriage *Great Yin* DOG
Happiness *Ridgepole* *Harmony* TIGER	Parents *Minister* OX	Life *Great Gate* RAT	Brothers *Wolf* *Virtue* PIG

Fig. 22. Purple Palace fate-calculation star chart

are no stars in a palace corresponding to the month or decade under question, the star in the opposite palace is then examined because it is considered to be a mirror of the palace being analyzed. For example, if the Wealth Palace in figure 22 represents the current year for an individual but has no stars, we can assume that the Ridgepole and Harmony Stars in the Happiness Palace will exert strong influence on the year in question. We know that the Ridgepole Star rewards leadership and the Harmony Star rewards modesty, which suggests that a modest leader will have a prosperous year.

5. Nine-Star divination

In this form of divination, calculations are conducted with a Nine-Star chart similar to the Guardian Stars of Eight-House *fengshui* (see table 9). Thus, each star has a Luo number as well as a five-phase value. However, in this system each star also has a designated color. Furthermore, the five phases correspond to the five "moving" stars (the visible planets) of the night sky. So, for example, Kan, or the One-White Star, corresponds to Mercury (the Water Star) because the phase of the Luo number

XUN 4-green	LI 9-purple	KUN 2-black
ZHEN 3-jade	5-yellow	DUI 7-red
GEN 8-white	KAN 1-white	QIAN 6-white

Fig. 23. A Nine-Star chart

1 is water. Li, or the Nine-Purple Star, corresponds to Mars (the Fire Star) because the phase of the Luo number 9 is fire. Zhen, or the Three-Jade Star, corresponds to Jupiter (the Wood Star) because the phase of the Luo number 3 is wood. And Dui, the Seven-Red Star, corresponds to Venus (the Metal Star), because the phase of the Luo number 7 is metal. The correspondence between the nine stars and the eight trigrams is illustrated in figure 23.

Divination is conducted by following the nine stars as they rove, or "fly," like their planetary counterparts, through the Nine Palaces according to the sequence of numbers in the Luo Writing. Since there are nine numbers, there are nine cycles of stars. Each cycle represents the "flying" of each number in each square of the Luo Writing from its original position to the next square in the sequence. In figure 24, the first year is the first palace, the second year is the second palace, and so on, until the ninth palace. The tenth year then returns to the first palace as the cycle starts over. When divining, stars of the colors purple and white are auspicious, while the colors jade, green, yellow, and black are inauspicious. This form of astrology is called flying star, flying heaven, and flying palace astrology, and its application will be illustrated in the following related system.

6. Flying Star *fengshui*

The principles governing Flying Star *fengshui* are very similar to Flying Star astrology. Called *Xuankong feixing*, or Mysterious Void Flying Star, it is a form of Compass School *fengshui* that is quite popular in the West. Unlike Eight-House *fengshui*, the flying star system also takes the passage of time into account. This school of *fengshui* believes that the flow of energy in the universe is not static but changes with the flow of time. The stars of Flying Star *fengshui* "fly" through a fixed sequence of temporal changes based on a cycle of twenty years, three of which form one epoch of the so-called tri-epoch (three cycles equal one epoch, and three epochs equals one great roving year of 180 years). When necessary, the changes can be based on shorter cycles of a year, or even only one month. Because the cycle of transformation changes every twenty years (or every year or every month), the position of each star also changes periodically.

The Eighth Cycle of the Lower Epoch began on February 4, 2004, and will continue until February 3, 2023. This cycle is governed by the Eighth Palace (see fig. 24), therefore the number 8 is in the central hall of the palace, and Eight-White is the ruling star (also called the prevailing star). In this palace, One-White is in the west and Six-White is in the east. These are auspicious directions for any house built in this twenty-year cycle. Another way of calculating good fortune based on the flying stars is dependent on observation of the relevant water star location. By water star is meant the direction the house faces, as opposed to the mountain star, which is the direction that backs up to the house. As you have already learned, traditionally a Chinese house sits with its back to a protective mountain with the land sloping away in front so that water might meander past and pool in front. Typically, then, the front of a house faces the lower ground of the site. If a house built in 2005 faces south, then based on the Eighth Cycle, the water star is Three-Jade. When this star flies, that is, when number 3 is in the central hall, the surrounding halls appear as in the Third Palace

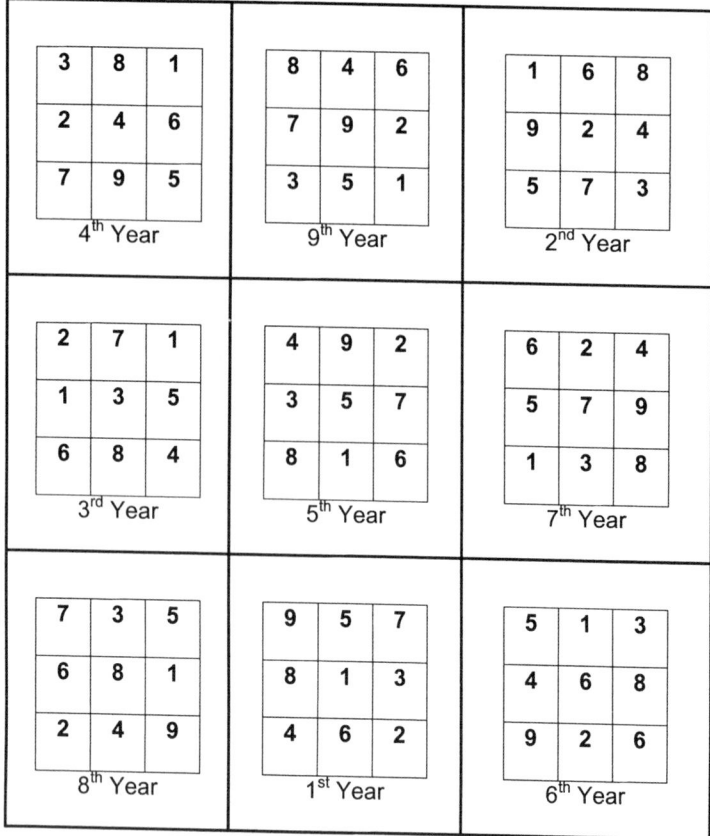

Fig. 24. The Nine Palaces

(see fig. 24). So One-White is in the east, Six-White is in the northeast, and Eight-White is in the north. These are also lucky directions. For the Eighth Cycle house, where Eight-White is the ruling star, Nine-Purple (because 9 follows 8) represents the future and Seven-Red (because 7 precedes 8) represents the past. Some *fengshui* masters will advise that the water star be located in the northwest and the mountain star in the southeast so that the back of the house is sitting in the past and the front is facing the future.

As mentioned above, the stars encountered in Purple Palace fate-calculation are not real stars in the Chinese sky, but are simply names of auspice based mainly on five-phase conjunctions. The same is true of both Nine-Star divination and Flying Star *fengshui*. Thus, none of these types of divination can be considered authentic astrology. China does indeed possess forms of divination based on actual celestial bodies. However, since actual celestial bodies form patterns and configurations in the sky, the interpretation of those images falls under my category of "augury," discussed in the next chapter.

CHAPTER 6

Augury, or Divination by Portentous Signs

I have borrowed the term "augury" to represent the practice of divination that interprets images or signs. In ancient Rome the augur observed the flight of birds in order to determine the will of the gods. In ancient China divination by sign also originated from the people's observation of things in the phenomenal world, but more particularly from the portentous appearance of such signs. As I mentioned in the introduction, divination by turtle is one of the oldest methods in China. With the cracking of plastrons or scapulae, one can determine good or bad fortune by observing the portentous appearance of the crack.

However, there are many other types of signs that could be used for divination. In addition to shell and bone cracks, the Chinese people recognize all manner of portents in the natural world. For example, Chinese astral divination is based on the character and position of the stars and other heavenly bodies in the sky at a given time, so it is also classified as augury. The divination methods of physiognomy, palmistry, and oneiromancy (dream interpretation), which are conducted based on particular (and especially peculiar) aspects of the human body or the different functions thus displayed, are also types of augury. Finally, a form of onomancy (divination by the letters of a name), called "fathoming characters," can be categorized as augury because the emphasis is on decoding the meaning of characters by means of their component elements. Since pyro-osteomancy was discussed in some detail in chapter 2, our discussion of augury will begin with astral divination.

Astral Divination

Chinese astral divination involves observing the movement, position, color, and brightness of heavenly bodies, and their relationship to each other, to determine the auspicious or inauspicious nature of human affairs. Divination by the Wood Star, for example, determines fortune according to the movement of Jupiter (also known as the Year Star in ancient China). If Jupiter is bright, with a yellow center, the world will be at peace. The direct movement of Jupiter represents humaneness. When Jupiter is out of sync, people will encounter difficulties. When it moves in spring, there will be agricultural disasters. When it progresses and retrogresses, the region it shines upon cannot fall. The color of the five moving stars (Venus, Jupiter, Mercury, Mars, and Saturn) is also portentous: white indicates mourning and drought, red indicates the military, green indicates grief and flood, black indicates illness and death, and yellow means good fortune. The silk manuscripts excavated at Mawangdui in 1973 included a Five-Star divination manual, which is a record of ancient Chinese astral divination dating to before the second century BCE.

Meteoromancy

Meteoromancy is the observation of the direction and strength of winds, and of the shapes of clouds and types of comet. Since its diviner senses the winds of the four directions and the four corners in order to determine good and bad fortune, it is similar to the palace of nine halls and the eight trigrams. In the *History of the Later Han*, there are biographies of the various diviners, including a number of those skilled in prognostication by observation of the winds. Lang Zong is worthy of mention because he was also well versed in theories of *Zhou Changes* fate-calculation. His skill was in such demand that he could make a living by charging for his services, and Emperor An Di (r. 107–126) eventually appointed him prefect of Wu. There was once the sudden appearance of a fierce wind in Wu, and Lang Zong predicted that extensive fires would rage in the capital. The time of his prediction was noted, and envoys were sent to investigate. His prophecy was verified when his messengers discovered large-scale fires in the city.

The first mention of this category of divination in the historical record is a passage from the *Records of the Grand Historian* (chap. 27). It mentions a meteorologist named Wei Xian who observed the weather on the first day of the year in order to predict the outcome of the year's harvest. One facet of his observations was based on wind direction, as summarized in table 13. For example, "On the first *jia* day of the new year, if the wind comes from the east, that is beneficial for the silkworm mulberry. However, if the wind comes from the west, and there are yellow clouds at sunrise, that is bad fortune." The auspice attached to the eight directions in these prognostications is probably based to some extent upon empirical observation. That is, winds from the maritime provinces in the northeast would likely bring quenching rains, whereas winds from the semiarid Tibetan plateau in the southwest would bring drought. On the other hand, there is a greater likelihood that five-phase correlations are involved.

In the following related passage from chapter 27 of the *Records of the Grand Historian,* it is not wind but the people's voices that are the basis for divination. This passage will serve to clarify how the five phases interact with winds to determine auspice. "At the beginning of the year, if the sky is clear and bright, then listen to the voices of the people. If the note of their voices is *gong,* then the harvest will be good and auspicious. If the note is *shang,* there will be war. The *zhi* note means drought. The *yu* note means floods. If the note is *jue,* the harvest will be poor." Table 14 juxtaposes the five phases, the five notes of the pentatonic scale, the predictions, and the directions.

Thus, the direction of fire is south, and south predicts drought in both table 13 and table 14. The phase of west is metal, the element of weapons, and the direction west in both tables predicts warfare. West is also the direction of most barbarian incursions in the Han dynasty. The direction of wood is east (and southeast; see fig. 16), and east or

TABLE 13. WIND DIRECTION AND HARVEST PREDICTIONS

Wind Direction	Prediction
South	Major drought
Southwest	Minor drought
West	There will be war.
Northwest	Great beans ripen; slight rains fall; a call to arms
North	Medium harvest
Northeast	Superior harvest
East	Major floods
Southeast	There is plague among the people, and harvests are poor.

TABLE 14. FIVE-PHASE WIND DIRECTION CORRELATIONS

Five Phases	Wind Direction	Five Notes	Predictions
Wood	East	*jue* (mi)	Poor harvest
Fire	South	*zhi* (sol)	Drought
Earth	Center	*gong* (do)	Good harvest
Metal	West	*shang* (re)	War
Water	North	*yu* (la)	Floods

southeast both predict poor harvests. Since meteoromancy bases prediction on all aspects of meteorology, including clouds and wind, it is the particular directional character of *qi*, the vital energy of the cosmos, which is the subject of scrutiny here.

Divination by the Human Body

Conducting divination based on the natural condition of the body or changes that have some bearing on the individual's body is very popular around the world. Chinese physiognomy is similar to popular forms elsewhere, but other methods of anatomical divination reflect Chinese traditional culture and thought.

1. Physiognomy

    Face reading has a long history in China. Traditionally, all sages in ancient China were endowed with extraordinary physical features that were signs of their power and virtue. In the *Discourses Weighed in the Balance*, for example, we read that Zhuan Xu was marked with the earth branch for "seven" on his brow; Emperor Ku had double teeth; the Great Yu, founder of the Xia dynasty, had ears with three orifices. As for Confucius, the most popular of all sages, the crown of his head was sunken, his lips were like a cow's, and his head was covered with dark bumps.

    Chinese physiognomy has extremely systematic and meticulous theories; when conducting a reading, each portion of the face has a formulation. The means of conducting physiognomy generally begins with inspecting bone structure. Human faces can be divided into the three sections—top (forehead), middle (eyes and nose), and bottom (mouth and chin)—whose length must be taken into account when a reading is taken. Ideally the face should be divided evenly among the three sections. The two frontal bones of the forehead, the two temples, and the two lateral bones of the face are called the six mansions. The upper jaw, the chin, the cheekbones, and the nose are called the five mountains. The six mansions and the five mountains must all be well developed before one can be dignified and attain wealth and honor. A complete reading of the face also includes a reading of the back of the head, chiefly the occipital bone.

Secondly, the size and character of the sense organs are analyzed. For example, the ears are well-known indicators of fortune. In general, the larger the ears, the greater the fortune. Thus, ears that "catch the wind" indicate that a person will love the pursuit of knowledge and will be quite enterprising but will also be stubborn. People with thick ears and well-defined earlobes will be strong-willed, trustworthy, and capable of attaining great wealth. If a woman's earlobes are large and prominent, her husband will have great fortune. On the other hand, thin ears herald bad fortune. Such people will be impetuous and will spend money without restraint. If a woman's ears are thin like paper, her husband will surely die. If the ears rise high up on the head, the person will be famous. If both ears droop to the shoulders, one's nobility will be unprecedented. Thus, the Buddha's long earlobes were proof of his status as a prince.

In addition to the three divisions of the face and the disposition of its features, another important facial examination is based on the same Twelve Palaces that govern fortune in Purple Palace divination (see fig. 25, where the palaces are duplicated for each side of the face). For example, the Life Palace is located above the nose, between the eyebrows. If this area is bright like a mirror, one's erudition will be comprehensive. Conversely, if the eyebrows intrude upon the Life Palace, such a person will be of low social status, his life will be chaotic, he will be forced to leave his native place, and he will be fated to mourn his wife's death. The Marriage Palace is located beyond the outside corner of each eye. If this

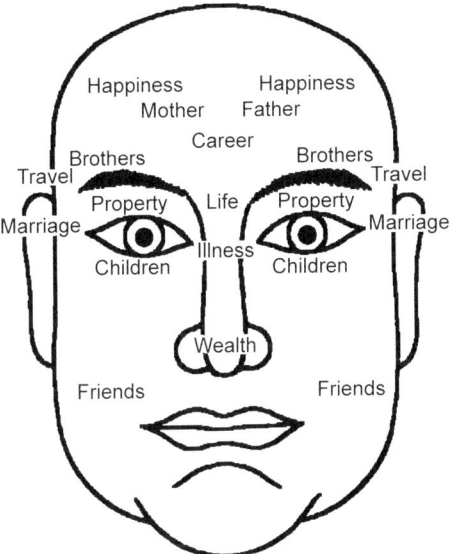

Fig. 25. The Twelve Palaces of physiognomy

area is smooth and bright, then such people will be faithful to their spouses. On the other hand, men with pitted skin in the Marriage Palace will divorce often. If a mole grows here, such men will be immoral. The Illness Palace is located below the Life Palace on the bridge of the nose. If the skin in this area is lustrous, one will be happy and live until a ripe old age. If the color is cloudy, on the other hand, one will often encounter hardship.

2. Other forms of anatomical divination

    Besides physiognomy, there are also forms of divination based on the twitching of the eyelids, ringing of the ears, sneezing, and so on. When divining by eye-twitching, the most important factor is when the eyelid twitches. Table 15 indicates the governing factor when either eye twitches at a particular time of the day.

3. Oneiromancy

    Dream interpretation also has a long tradition in ancient China. A famous mythical record of oneiromancy was the basis of the

TABLE 15. DIVINATION BY EYE-TWITCHING

Double Hour	Left Eye	Right Eye
11:00 p.m.–1:00 a.m.	Nobility	Food and wine
1:00–3:00 a.m.	Grieving	Human longing
3:00–5:00 a.m.	Travelers	Luck
5:00–7:00 a.m.	Nobility	Peace
7:00–9:00 a.m.	Guests coming	Injury
9:00–11:00 a.m.	Food and wine	Misfortune
11:00 a.m.–1:00 p.m.	Satisfaction	Misfortune
1:00–3:00 p.m.	Good fortune	Happiness
3:00–5:00 p.m.	Wealth	Writing
5:00–7:00 p.m.	news	guests going
7:00–9:00 p.m.	other matters	food and wine
9:00–11:00 p.m.	nobility	official matters

overthrow of a dynasty. The last king of the Xia dynasty was Jie, a tyrant famous for his wickedness. One night he dreamed that there were two suns in the sky, one in the east and one in the west. There was a struggle, and the western sun was victorious. This dream was told to spies by the neglected queen and eventually reported to Tang the Successful. The next day Tang led his troops around to the western border of the city before beginning his attack. Because Jie believed that his dream was about to come true, he fled before a blow had been struck, and Tang became the first king of the Shang dynasty.

Manuals of dream interpretation are often attributed to famous people. The following examples of dream interpretation are all taken from the contemporary edition of a traditional manual called *The Duke of Zhou Interprets Dreams*. If one dreams of people descending from heaven, that is great good fortune, as are dreams of ascending to heaven, which portend the birth of an honorable son. A dream of hot weather portends war, while dreams of rain portend calamity. A dream of earthquake portends emigration. Dreams of buying land, breaking ground, and entering a house are greatly auspicious, whereas a dream of earth covering the body portends great misfortune. If one dreams of digging in the ground, then one will assume an official position in the future. If a man dreams of a door opening, then his wife will have an affair. A dream of knocking on someone's door is very auspicious. If one dreams of gates or openings, he will worry about descendants.

If a young man dreams about a girl's bedroom, then his love will be consummated. When a businessman dreams about a girl's bedroom, then his business will thrive. It is an unlucky omen for a man to dream that his bedroom is filled with women. When a man or woman dreams of an empty bedroom, they will lose their spouse or lover. When a woman dreams of a stranger's bedroom, disaster looms. When an old man dreams of a young girl's bedroom, he is about to die. When a man dreams about taking his clothes off, it implies that his life is too extravagant and unrestrained. On the other hand, when a woman dreams that she is removing her clothes, it means that her family will be joyful. If a man dreams that his wife takes off her clothes, then he will soon discover her secret.

Divination by Deciphering Ideographs

Deciphering ideographs is a form of divination unique to China. The diviner chooses one or more Chinese characters, separates them into their constituent elements, and then determines good or bad fortune based on deductions suggested by those elements. In order to understand this form of divination, it is necessary to know how Chinese characters are composed. Each Chinese character contains one or more components, called radicals, each of which has its own category of meaning. For example, tree names normally include the "wood" pictograph, and bodies of water (lakes, rivers, ponds) include the "water" pictograph. Ideographs derive their meaning from the combination of two pictographs. Thus, a hand covering the eyes forms *kan*, which means "to gaze into the distance." A person leaning against a tree forms *xiu*, which means "to rest" (see fig. 26). Folk diviners, based on their elaborations of these meanings, created a unique form of divination called fathoming, dissecting, or cleaving characters.

History records many masters of fathoming characters, such as Xie Shi of the Song dynasty, who was perhaps the most famous practitioner of this form of divination. According to one story, Xie Shi

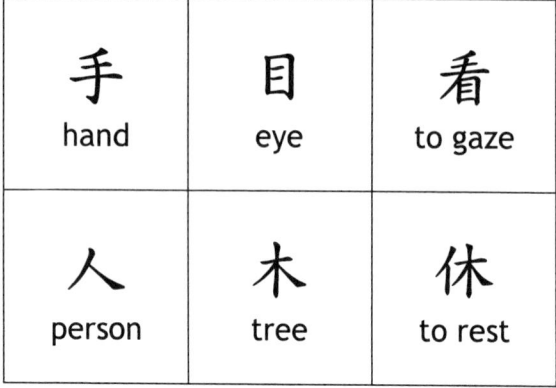

Fig. 26. Chinese characters

Fig. 27. Chinese characters

started his practice in his native town of Chengdu and slowly gained popularity due to the accuracy of his predictions. One day a malicious client brought him the character *nai*, composed of only two strokes of the brush, which would normally have been considered too simple to base a prediction upon. However, his skills were so extraordinary that he produced the following fortune: "The character *nai* is the incomplete writing of the character *ji*, 'to attain.' In your entire life you will never be able to attain your goal" (see fig. 27).

In the year 1119, Xie Shi set up shop in the capital, and his fame eventually reached the emperor. Inviting him to the palace, the emperor secretly had his son, the crown prince, write down a character for Xie to analyze. Based on the character he was shown (*tai*), Xie subsequently divined: "This means the emperor." The emperor asked why, and Xie replied: "The dot at the bottom of *tai* indicates the

Augury, or Divination by Portentous Signs

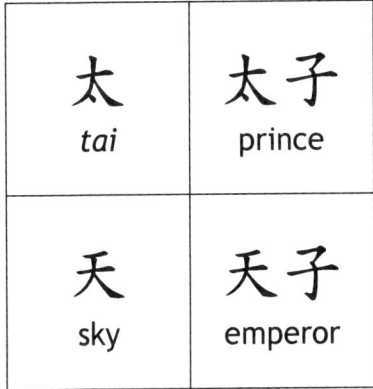

Fig. 28. Chinese characters

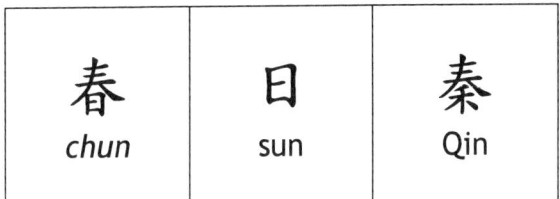

Fig. 29. Chinese characters

crown prince (*taizi*). As his sun ascends to the top of the sky (*tian*), doesn't the prince become the emperor?" (see fig. 28).

Another story tells us that many years later, another emperor consulted Xie Shi, giving him the character *chun*. He responded: "The top of the character *qin* is too heavy; it bears down upon the sun so there is no light." In this manner he secretly admonished Qin Hui, who was trying to monopolize power (see fig. 29).

When Qin Hui got word of this affront, he was enraged and devised a plan for framing Xie Shi so that he was banished to the frontier. Then, Qin Hui secretly dispatched a soldier to follow him. En route to his place of exile, Xie encountered a woman fortune-teller living in the mountains whose sign advertised the art of fathoming characters. He was compelled to approach her and write the character *xie* (his surname) for her to analyze. The woman fortune-

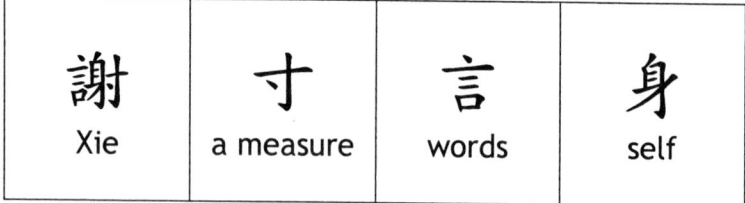

Fig. 30. Chinese characters

Fig. 31. Chinese characters

Fig. 32. Chinese characters

teller laughed and said, "A magician, not worth fathoming." Xie Shi invited her to explain, and she replied, "He measures words to establish himself in society. If this is not a magician, then what is it?" (see fig. 30).

Xie Shi was amazed, so he wrote down another character *shi* (stone), his given name. The fortune-teller remarked, "This character is very bad luck. When stone encounters a weapon, it is smashed to pieces. The person following you is a soldier" (see fig. 31). As soon as Xie Shi heard this, he knew his life was about to end. With a great sigh he informed the fortune-teller that he could also fathom characters and wished to reciprocate by analyzing a character for her. She smiled

Augury, or Divination by Portentous Signs

and answered, "As I stand here, I am a character." Xie Shi looked at her, stupefied, and said: "A person standing next to a mountain; can it be that you are an immortal?" (see fig. 32). The woman laughed and said nothing, then transformed into a wisp of cloud and disappeared. According to legend, Xie Shi was also transformed in this fashion by an immortal.

In this chapter I have included only those forms of divination where images or pictures of some kind could be visualized. In the next chapter, I discuss sortilege, or divination by random selection. Although this category may also seem to relate to numbers, those numbers are titular only and have no inherent mystical meaning.

CHAPTER 7

Sortilege, or Divination by Choosing from Lots

Sortilege is divination by the drawing of lots. Humans have probably been using lots to make decisions since they were first able to count. Lots are objects such as stones or sticks placed in a container and drawn or cast at random. The simplest technique requires stones of different colors or sticks of different lengths ("drawing straws"). A more complex technique requires that the stones or sticks be inscribed with meaningful symbols such as numbers or words. A die, or pair of dice, is a lot-casting instrument. The English word lottery is derived from "lot" and means a system of distributing prizes based on the drawing of lots. The lots in this case are simply a sequence of numbers drawn from a series of digits.

In China, lots have been used since ancient times. The Qin dynasty tomb of a diviner—the same tomb that contained the *Guicang* divination manual—included two different types of dice, a bamboo box of counting sticks, and a divining board. In the following analysis I begin by looking at the earliest textual evidence of the farmer's almanac, a form of divination whereby the individual chooses the proper day for conducting activities from a calendar listing lucky and unlucky days. I then proceed to a discussion of stick-sorting techniques where the diviner shakes a container of numbered sticks until one emerges. The number on the stick will then correspond to a particular fortune in a book.

Divination by Selecting Days

Hemerology, or divining the proper day on which to conduct activities, is ancient in China. The Han dynasty *Records of the Grand Historian* says this about the tradition: "In ancient times, when the former kings managed the affairs of the state, they dared not undertake their duties without first consulting the turtle and milfoil to ascertain the proper day and month. And only after determining the correct hour and day were they able to move house and home" (chap. 127). Even earlier, in the fifth century BCE book of *Mozi*, the following story is recorded: "Mozi was traveling north to Qi and met a diviner of days who said: 'God will kill the black dragon on this day in the north. Since the master's complexion is black, he cannot travel north.' Mozi paid no attention and continued north. At the River Zi he could proceed no further and thus returned" (12).

Until recently, our understanding of ancient hemerology was limited to the few references in classical texts such as these. However, in 1975, a Qin dynasty tomb was uncovered that contained two groups of bamboo strips that have been identified as *rishu* (daybooks). This is the earliest known example of a type of book that is in common use in China today—virtually every household in China owns a copy of the *tongshu* (almanac).

The contents of these daybooks are of two basic types. One type, of which the *jianchu* divination system is representative, specifies the general auspice of the days of the year. In this calendrical divination system, years are counted according to twelve unique qualities. Months are identified by lunar lodge of the new moon. Days are counted sexidecimally, but auspice is apportioned solely according to the earth branch designation of each day (of which there are only twelve). So, days that share the same earth branch within a given month share the same auspice. However, auspice for each of the twelve branch days changes each month based on the two emblematic series attached to them (see day auspice class and quality in table 16). For example, all A-branch days in the eleventh month (when the new moon lodges in the constellation Dou, or the Southern Ladle) are classed as "weak" with the quality of "knotty." However, in the twelfth month (when the new moon is in the constellation Xu, or Beard), all A-branch days are classified as "bursting" with the quality of "luxuriant." Table 17 organizes the information in approximately the same format as it appears on thirteen of the excavated bamboo slips.

In addition to the information appearing in table 16, appended to each column of auspice emblems is another short prognosticatory

TABLE 16. DAY AUSPICE

Number in the Series	Year Cycle	Classification of Day Auspice	Quality of Day Auspice
1	Established (jian)	Weak	Knotty
2	Removed (chu)	Victorious	Sunny
3	Full	Established	Joined
4	Level	Trapped	Harmful
5	Set	Broken	Cloudy
6	Controlled	Level	Successful
7	Broken	Peaceful	Sunny Beyond
8	Dangerous	Empty	Harmful Beyond
9	Complete	Seated	Cloudy Beyond
10	Received	Covered	[damaged slip]
11	Open	Successful	Double Bright
12	Shut	Bursting	Luxuriant

TABLE 17. *CHU* YEAR ALMANAC

12	11	10	9	8	7	6	5	4	3	2	1	Day/Month
Bursting	(see table 16 for these values)										**Weak**	CLASS
	L	K	J	I	H	G	F	E	D	C	B	**A**	11 *Dou*
A	L	K	J	I	H	G	F	E	D	C	**B**	12 *Xu*
B	**A**	L	K	J	I	H	G	F	E	D	C	1 *Ying*
C	B	**A**	L	K	J	I	H	G	F	E	D	2 *Kui*
D	C	B	**A**	L	K	J	I	H	G	F	E	3 *Wei*
E	D	C	B	**A**	L	K	J	I	H	G	F	4 *Bi*
F	E	D	C	B	**A**	L	K	J	I	H	G	5 *Dong*
G	F	E	D	C	B	**A**	L	K	J	I	H	6 *Liu*
H	G	F	E	D	C	B	**A**	L	K	J	I	7 *Zhang*
I	H	G	F	E	D	C	B	**A**	L	K	J	8 *Jiao*
J	I	H	G	F	E	D	C	B	**A**	L	K	9 *Shi*
K	J	I	H	G	F	E	D	C	B	**A**	L	10 *Xin*
Luxuriant	(see table 16 for these values)										**Knotty**	QUALITY

text that raises specific issues that the diviner might take into account when planning activities. For example, in the eleventh month of the Chu year, every A-branch day is a "knotty" day. Under the knotty day emblem at the bottom of the bamboo slip appears this text: "On knotty days, any business undertaken without conducting sacrificial offerings will be cause for regret. If a son is born there will be no younger brother, or if there is a younger brother he will die. As for lodgers, they will take over the master's house." In the third month of the Chu year, every A-branch day is a "cloudy beyond" day (9th branch). Beneath the cloudy beyond day emblem is appended this prognosticatory text: "On cloudy beyond days it is beneficial to conduct sacrifices. Conducting business and acquiring goods will both be auspicious. Going beyond the wilds is not advised."

The examples given above from the *jianchu* divination system are general predictions of the auspice of days in a whole year. Because the excavated tomb contains the almanac based on the Chu year cycle (and none of the other years in the twelve-year cycle), scholars speculate that the deceased person buried there was born in the year of Chu, and these tables represented his own personal horoscope. If this is indeed the case, then the *jianchu* daybooks would better accord with astrology, which depends on the circumstances of a person's birth. The Chu year might then be comparable to the Year of the Ox (second in the series) in the system based on the twelve animals. The *jianchu* system would then differ from *tongshu* almanacs whose descriptions of auspice pertain to all people, regardless of year of birth.

Following the *jianchu* and similar daybooks is another category of texts that are arranged according to divination topic rather than days. Activities included are disease, travel, marriage, childbirth, dreams, and building projects, among many others. An example of an item under the heading of illness is as follows: "Illness that falls on a 7- or 8-stem day is inflicted by a ghost from outside that kills the young. It was acquired through dog meat or fresh eggs of white color. If the illness is more serious on a 1- or 2-stem day, there will be relief on a 3-stem day, and final recovery on a 4-stem day. Otherwise, great difficulty resides in the west, for the Year Star [Jupiter] is in the west, and the color of white is death." In this particular section of the daybooks, auspice is apportioned according to the heaven stem designation of each day rather than by the twelve earth branch days of the *jianchu* almanac.

In the same set of bamboo slips discussed above are four similar passages for a total of five texts that outline the illnesses that fall on pairs of heaven stem days. With this set of prognostications we are better able to understand the rationale behind the designation of aus-

TABLE 18. HEAVEN STEMS AND FIVE-PHASE CORRELATIONS

Stem Pairs	Phase	Direction
1, 2	Wood	East
3, 4	Fire	South
5, 6	Earth	Center
7, 8	Metal	West
9, 10	Water	North

pice. That is because the text is quite transparent in its reliance on five-phase correlations for meaning. The ten heaven stems correspond to the five phases as illustrated in table 18. Based on the mutual generation and conquest orders of the five phases, the stem pairs in their numerical succession generate each other. That is, stems 1 and 2 produce stems 3 and 4 because wood feeds fire, and so on. In the passage above, the 7- or 8-stem day illness comes from the west, not only because Jupiter, a star of misfortune, is in the western sky, but also because stems 7 and 8 are correlated with the direction west. Stems 7 and 8 belong to the metal phase, which cuts wood. Since wood is the characteristic of the stem pair 1 and 2, therefore the illness gets worse on those days. However, the quality of the stem pair 3 and 4 is fire. Since fire melts metal, the illness is finally quelled on stem days 3 and 4.

Another subject of divination in this second category of daybooks is home construction. Here one can find favorable dates for starting construction in addition to prohibitions regarding the building of houses. For example, on stem days 7 and 8 of the three months of spring, on stem days 9 and 10 of the three months of summer, on stem days 1 and 2 of the three months of autumn, and on stem days 3 and 4 of the three months of winter, one should not commence construction. If this prohibition is violated, the master of the house will either die or become ill. In other passages we are told on what days it is dangerous to put in doors and windows. Still another section advises which days are best for breaking ground.

Divination by Sorting Bamboo Sticks

The sorting of bamboo lots is a form of divination most commonly found in Daoist and Buddhist temples. There, worshippers have access to a bamboo tube holding approximately a hundred numbered sticks, which they may shake to cast out a single stick. The number on the randomly obtained stick corresponds to the proper fortune. The fortunes involved usually are attributed to ancient sages, including the Daoist immortal, Lü Dongbin; the Buddhist goddess of mercy, Guanyin; the Han dynasty physician, Hua Tuo; the Daoist god of war, Guan Di; and various characters from the Ming dynasty novel *Outlaws of the Marsh*. The following fortunes are all derived from the sorting of numbered bamboo sticks as outlined above; however, in each case the numbers correspond to different divination manuals.

1. Patriarch Lü's medicinal lots

    In the Tang dynasty we are told there lived a man named Lü Dongbin who had failed twice in his attempt to pass the civil service exam. One day in the capital, while waiting for a pot of millet to boil for his meal, he fell asleep and had a dream. In his dream he passed the exam, became prime minister, and married the daughter of a wealthy family. However, he incurred the jealousy of court officials whose slander resulted in his imprisonment and eventual ruin. As he lay dying, he awoke to find that the millet had yet to finish cooking. Realizing that his goals for riches and fame in this life were no more consequential than those of his dream, he left his family and became a Daoist adept. He is credited with founding the Golden Elixir sect of Daoism and is known as Lü the Patriarch. He eventually joined the group of Daoist deities called the Eight Immortals. Lü Dongbin is the patron saint of merchants, pharmacists, and scholars.

    Lü's medicinal lots are divided into five categories: husband, wife, children, in-laws, and miscellaneous topics. For example, slip #85 under the category of "husband" reads as follows: "Dispel anger and your worries will disappear. Be calm and collect Sweet Dew to insure that your sadness is naught. Take 10 grams of Job's Tears, 10 grams of peach pits, 10 grams of tuckahoe, 10 grams of water plantain, 10 grams of flower pollen, seven parts of cornel, 10 grams of lucid asparagus, 5 grams of *caojie*; add two bowls of water and boil down to one cup. Makes five doses." The medicinal lot is a popular form of bamboo lot whose fortune text is followed by an herbal prescription. When the seeker obtains the advice from the spirits, he may simultaneously receive a concrete prescription for his health and thus increase the efficacy of the lot's guidance.

2. Guanyin's lots

Guanyin is the most well known of all Chinese goddesses. She is a bodhisattva, which are enlightened beings who have put off entering Buddhist paradise in order to help others attain enlightenment. It is believed that any person who recites her name during a time of trouble will be saved, which explains the origin of her full name, Guanshiyin ("observing the sounds of the world"). She is known in the West as the Buddhist goddess of mercy. Guanyin's bamboo lots number one hundred and include thirty fortunes of great merit, fifty-five of medium merit, and fifteen of low merit. The content of the fortunes includes both verses and hexagram images and deals with all aspects of daily life, including the human body, the house, marriage, birth, wealth, farming and sericulture, husbandry, moving, travel, illness, and lawsuits. The hundred Guanyin lots are divided into twelve palaces according to the twelve earth branches. The quality of persuasion is quite straightforward. For example, the verse of fortune #14 reads as follows: "Just like the white crane flies out of its cage, you flee your confinement and the road is clear ahead. Obstructions disappear in all directions; your promotion goes straight up to the ninth palace." The explanation of the image and the fortune are as follows:

> The image of the white crane fleeing its cage indicates that what begins with sorrow will end with good fortune. Fortunes are: for the home there will be unrest, for your person there will be a promise kept, for your prosperity transactions will be concluded, for marriage there will be a union, for pregnancy there will be a son born, for seeking someone a person will appear, for agriculture there will be advantage in

autumn, for husbandry there will be loss, for travel there will be obstruction, lawsuits will be harmonious, moving will be auspicious, illness will be cured, burials will be auspicious. Fourth Palace.

Finally, the fortune tells the story of Jiang Ziya to explain the image of promotion. Jiang Ziya is better known as Lü Shang, or Grand Duke Wang, who became minister and general to King Wen, posthumous founder of the Zhou dynasty.

3. Guan Di's lots

Guan Yü (162–219 CE) was a famous and beloved general from the Three Kingdoms period who exemplified the Confucian ethics of loyalty, respect, and sincerity. After he died in battle, the people built shrines throughout the country to honor him. Eventually he was deified as Guan Di, the Chinese god associated with war (but not in the sense of Mars or Ares). He is also regarded by some Chinese as the god of wealth. Guan Di's lots number one hundred, including three lots of highest fortune, nine of great good fortune, fourteen of good fortune, eight of medium fortune, one of above average fortune, thirty-eight of average fortune, and twenty-seven of lesser fortune. The text of each fortune includes a topic and a verse, in addition to such information as "oracular confirmations," "the sage's intentions," "Su Dongpo's explanations," "the Jade Immortal's glosses," and so on.

Let us take a closer look at Guan Di's fortune #3. The topic is: "Jia Yi meets Emperor Wendi of the Han." It is a medium fortune. The verse reads: "Birth and position are natural, clothing and food follow along. It is useless to toil and trouble about such things. But if one is filial and fraternal, loyal and trustworthy, good fortune will come and misfortune will not intrude." The explanation reads: "With this fortune it is necessary to stick to the old ways; one cannot thirst after things. But if one remains loyal and righteous, he will achieve stability. One must rely on filial, fraternal, loyal, and trustworthy behavior, and he will receive happiness and riches as a result. If one seeks to take by force or impose upon, on the contrary he will attract unexpected misfortune. If the seeker accords with reason and is content with his lot, he will have good fortune." The paraphrase reads:

> Clothing and food are fated; birth and position are tied to a person's allotted life and cannot be coerced. It is useless to worry about them and advisable not to exceed one's bounds. One should attend to the basic virtues. With filial and fraternal behavior one attains the moral high ground; with loyalty and trustworthiness one can best handle life's duties. If one behaves in this manner, he will receive the appraisal and assistance of heaven. Happiness will gather and luck will be attained, you will be contented wherever you may be. All matters will bring good fortune and no misfortune will come your way. Everything depends on the rectification of behavior; you cannot turn your back on your true nature. Be prudent.

For a realistic description of a stick-sorting ceremony and reading, see the following account of a fortune-telling district in Hong Kong as recorded by Richard Smith.

Divination at the Huang Daxian Temple

> The god's name is Huang Daxian. He is a minor figure in a vast Chinese pantheon, unworthy of even the briefest mention in most standard reference works, and virtually unknown outside of Hong Kong. But he is considered particularly efficacious by his local constituents, who flock daily and in large numbers to his temple in Kowloon, both to pay their respects and to ask for his advice and assistance. The temple is large and ornate, built in the Qing imperial style, with yellow-tiled roofing, brightly-colored upper panels of red, blue and gold, and conventional Chinese symbols of cosmic power and good fortune, including depictions of dragons, paired protective lions at the front entrance, and auspicious calligraphic inscriptions on its large red pillars. The temple also has two prominently displayed donation boxes, which indicate explicitly that blessings come to those who give.

Sortilege, or Divination by Choosing from Lots

Huang Daxian is ensconced in the dark recesses of the main building, but the action is all outside. Dozens of worshippers, most of them women, are kneeling in prayer, bowing, burning incense, and offering oranges, bananas and other gifts of food. Some of the offerings are presented on long tables in front of the major gateways known as *pailou;* others are brought directly to the central courtyard. The air is thick with fragrant smoke that rises from dark metal incense burners and wafts gently throughout the temple complex. Within the courtyard, and on the periphery opposite the main hall, a number of worshippers kneel next to small, tube-shaped bamboo containers about ten inches tall and seven inches around. These containers are supplied by the temple, and each holds a hundred individually-numbered bamboo sticks, called *qian.* After offering devotions to Huang Daxian, each supplicant asks for his help in solving a particular problem. The worshipper then shakes the bamboo container in a downward motion until a single stick falls away from the rest. He or she then removes it, and casts a pair of crescent-shaped bamboo or wooden blocks called *jiao* to see if the stick selected was the "correct" one. These *jiao* are rounded on one side and flat on the other. If both blocks land flat side down on the ground, the answer is no; if one flat side is up and the other down, the answer is yes; if both flat sides land facing upward, it means that the god is laughing—try again.

Eventually the process yields a "yes," and the temple provides a handy printed message corresponding to the number written on the bamboo stick. This message consists of a simple, classical-style poem of four lines written in red ink on a small pink slip of paper. Each poem is identified with a famous culture hero of the past, such as the "creator" Pan Gu, who "opened up Heaven and Earth" (stick number 52), the philosopher Zhuang Zhou (Zhuangzi), who "dreamt he was a butterfly" (stick number 54), or the military strategist Zhuge Liang, who "planned the defeat of Cao Cao" (stick number 33). A booklet entitled *Huang Daxian lingqian* (The

Spiritual Sticks of Huang Daxian) can also be purchased, which provides poetic texts for all one hundred possibilities. The main commentary of this booklet explains the symbolism and meaning of each poem, while shorter commentaries provide appropriate answers to general questions regarding wealth, illness, marriage, travel, and so forth. Individuals in need of further guidance can consult a stable of fortune-tellers located down a series of stone steps in a wood-frame structure adjacent to the temple complex.

Concluding Remarks

In the "Appended Statements" commentary of the *Classic of Changes,* it is recorded that sage-king Fuxi "looked upward and contemplated the images in the heavens, then looked downward and contemplated the patterns on earth." Based on his observations, he invented the eight trigrams in order to communicate with the gods and gain mastery over the world. Then, armed with this knowledge, he and the sage-kings that followed him proceeded to invent the tools of civilization: nets for fishing, the bow and arrow for hunting, the plow for agriculture, boats for transportation, and so on. In this primitive worldview, divination was the first skill of the culture hero who could not have forged civilization out of the wilderness without "the light of the gods." From an anthropological point of view, such communication allowed the people to survive in a hostile world by instilling in them a superstitious awe for the potencies of nature. Flood and earthquake, no less than quenching rains and bountiful harvests, were sent by the gods.

As society progressed, the world would have become less mysterious and more "predictable," so divining intuitively by natural omens would have yielded to more complicated systems of augury that required the exercise of the human intellect. This accounts to some extent for the growing regularization of divination systems from the Shang dynasty until the height of metaphysical thinking in Han dynasty China. Yet one thing remained constant from the earliest examples of Neolithic divination to the most complicated forms of fate calculation: apparently, the gods speak to humans through the language of chance. Whether it is the chance occurrence of a natural phenomenon, the random generation of a sequence of numbers, a fortuitous date of birth, or simply a lucky draw, in all cases the divinity of the event lies strictly in its coincidence.

As mentioned in the introduction, the ancient diviners may have realized that the only way to insure that the king was not skewing the answer to his question was to seek complete randomness in the oracular response. However, what appears to us as random chance was considered divine intervention by the diviners. Eventually, the classical philosophers refined their understanding of chance: both ordered change and random change were aspects of the natural cycle. So, as divinatory systems progressed and as divination evolved into philosophy, the Chinese did their utmost to create a science of prediction so that fate and fortune might be distilled from within this crucible of unceasing change. That, of course, is the real theme of this study.

I have tried to give the reader some idea of how the evolution of divination procedures proceeded as Chinese culture matured. By necessity, a great deal of the discussion could give only a general view, and I had to be circumspect in the areas where finer distinctions could be made. At the same time, the reader can be assured of having received a comprehensive and up-to-date account of the origin and evolution of divination in China while also becoming knowledgeable about some of its most important practical applications. I could not be more clear or complete on the origin of divination in ancient China but, as more materials are uncovered by archaeological work, the terrain of ancient Chinese religion will certainly become clearer and more complete. I invite readers to continue their study of Chinese divination and hope that this simple map has inspired others to continue the journey.

Appendix
Chinese Spelling and Pronunciation

Chinese words are spelled according to the *pinyin* system of Mandarin romanization. *Pinyin* consonants are pronounced as in English, except for the following:

c	as in *cang*	pronounced like the *ts* of *its*
q	as in *qian*	pronounced like the *ch* in *chin*
x	as in *xiang*	pronounced like the *sh* in *she*
zh	as in *zhen*	pronounced like the English *j* (not the French *j*)
r	as in *ren*	pronounced like the *sure* in *pleasure*

Simple vowels have the following pronunciations:

a	as in *ma*	pronounced like the *o* in *hot*
e	as in *he*	pronounced like the *u* in *fudge*
i or yi	as in *qi*	pronounced like the *ee* in *cheese*
o	as in *bo*	pronounced like the *o* in *border*
u or wu	as in *kun*	pronounced like the *oo* in *woo*
ü or yu	as in *lü*	pronounced like the *ue* in *cue*
sibilant -i	as in *ci, si, zi*	pronounced like the *oo* in *book*
retroflex -i	as in *chi, shi, zhi, ri*	pronounced like the *ir* in *bird*

Further Reading

STUDIES OF CHINESE DIVINATION

Chemla, Karine, Donald Harper, and Marc Kalinowski, eds. *Divination et Rationalité en Chine Ancienne* (Vol. 21 of *Extrême-Orient, Extrême-Occident: Cahiers de Recherches Comparatives*). Saint-Denis, France: Presses Universitaires de Vincennes, 1999. A collection of articles by experts in the field of ancient Chinese thought, this book examines the relationship between divination and the history of scientific thought in the Shang, Zhou, and Han dynasties. It is not a study of divination in its own right but is an attempt to place the arts of divination in the context of other systems of rational discourse. Four of the nine chapters are in English.

De Woskin, Kenneth. *Doctors, Diviners and Magicians of Ancient China: Biographies of Fang-shih*. New York: Columbia University Press, 1983. A translation of selected biographies of "specialists in occult prescriptions" from three dynastic histories covering the first four centuries of the common era.

Ho, Peng Yoke. *Chinese Mathematical Astrology: Reaching Out to the Stars*. New York: RoutledgeCurzon, 2003. An excellent discussion of *liuren, dunjia*, and *taiyi* divination by one of the world's foremost scholars of ancient Chinese science.

Loewe, Michael. *Divination, Mythology and Monarchy in Han China*. Cambridge University Press, 1994. Loewe traces the major developments in the ideas of sovereignty along with some of their religious aspects, including the techniques used by emperors and others to forecast the future or to divine the present.

Nielson, Bent. *A Companion to Yi Jing Numerology and Cosmology: Chinese Studies of Images and Numbers from Han (202 BCE–220 CE) to Song (960–1279)*. New York: RoutledgeCurzon, 2003. Explanations of technical terms and various concepts related to the image and number tradition of the *Classic of Changes*, plus biographical and bibliographical information of scholars and their works.

Poo, Mu-chou. *In Search of Personal Welfare: A View of Ancient Chinese Religion*. Albany: State University of New York Press, 1998. Poo Mu-chou provides a historical investigation of religious beliefs in ancient China from the earliest period to the end of the Han dynasty. His overall concern is to try to reach the religious mentality of the ancient Chinese in the context of personal and daily experiences.

Smith, Richard J. *Fortune-Tellers and Philosophers: Divination in Traditional Chinese Society*. Boulder: Westview, 1991. The best general study in English on the subject of Chinese divination, in this book Richard Smith presents a historical overview of divination and examines various divinatory practices and their role in Qing society. In addition to geomancy, fate calculation, and shamanism, he analyzes in great detail the role of the *Classic of Changes* and its enormous influence on late imperial Chinese culture.

TRANSLATIONS OF THE TEXTS OF CHINESE DIVINATION

Aylward, Thomas F., tr. *The Imperial Guide to Feng Shui & Chinese Astrology: The Only Authentic Translation from the Original Chinese*. London: Watkins, 2007. A translation of the Qing dynasty (1644–1911) text, *Xieji bianfang shu* (Treatise on Harmonizing Times and Distinguishing Directions). Aylward's introduction to this scholarly translation is a comprehensive discussion of the structure of ancient Chinese cosmology.

Lynn, Richard John, tr. *The Classic of Changes: A New Translation of the I Ching as Interpreted by Wang Bi*. New York: Columbia University Press, 1994. This translation of Wang Bi's *Zhouyi zhu* is considered by many to be the best translation into English of the *Classic of Changes*.

Nylan, Michael, tr. *The Canon of Supreme Mystery, by Yang Hsiung. A Translation with Commentary of the* T'ai Hsüan Ching. Albany: State University of New York Press, 1993. As her teacher, Nathan Sivin, once remarked: "[Michael's] English version makes available a book that is superior to the *Yijing* for many of the uses to which Europeans have long put the latter, and that deserves to be known as a great work of literature as well as of philosophy."

Palmer, Martin, ed. and tr., with Mak Hin Chung, Kwok Man Ho, and Angela Smith. *T'ung Shu: An Ancient Chinese Almanac.*

Boston: Shambhala, 1986. This English translation of the traditional Chinese almanac allows the reader to choose lucky days for important occasions such as traveling, weddings, and moving house.

Rutt, Richard, tr. *The Book of Changes (Zhouyi)*. New York: RoutledgeCurzon, 2002. Although Father Rutt is not a scholar in the traditional mode, his translation and extensive annotation of the *Zhou Changes* is recognized as one of the most accurate renderings of the text based on the era that produced it. He also translates all passages from the *Zuo Commentary* and *Discourses of the States* that contain instances of milfoil divination.

Wilhelm, Richard, and Cary Baynes, trs. *The I Ching or Book of Changes*, with forward by C. G. Jung, and Preface to the Third Edition by Hellmut Wilhelm, Bollingen Series XIX. Princeton University Press, 1967. The Wilhelm/Baynes translation has become a cult classic in the English-speaking world of *Yijing* aficionados, owing partly to the imprimatur of the great psychologist, C. G. Jung.

STUDIES OF ANCIENT CHINESE COSMOLOGY

Allan, Sarah. *The Shape of the Turtle: Myth, Art, and Cosmos in Early China*. Albany: State University of New York Press, 1991. In this pioneering study, Sarah Allan analyzes the image of the turtle in Shang dynasty culture.

Graham, A. C. *Disputers of the Tao: Philosophical Argument in Ancient China*. La Salle, IL: Open Court, 1989. This book by a leading Western scholar of Chinese philosophy is one of the best comparative studies of classical Chinese philosophy in English. Graham's analysis of correlative cosmos building is especially enlightening.

Major, John S., tr. *Heaven and Earth in Early Han Thought: Chapters Three, Four, and Five of the* Huainanzi. Albany: State University of New York Press, 1993. The most complete translation into English of the seminal Daoist text, its introductory matter includes one of the best discussions available on Han dynasty cosmology.

Rosemont, Henry, ed. *Explorations in Early Chinese Cosmology*. Chico, CA: Scholars Press, 1984, reprinted 2006. A collection of important studies, all of which bear on one or another of the ideas discussed in the present volume.

OTHER RELEVANT STUDIES

Bennett, Steven J. "Patterns of Sky and Earth: A Chinese System of Applied Cosmology." *Chinese Science* 3 (March 1978): 1–26. This pioneering study of Form School *fengshui* is still one of the best sources available in English.

Field, Stephen. "The Numerology of Nine Star *Fengshui*: A *Hetu, Luoshu* Resolution of the Mystery of Directional Auspice." *Journal of Chinese Religion*, no. 27 (1999): 13–33. For those readers who would like to delve deeper into the numerology of Nine-Star *fengshui*, this article gives a detailed description of the formula for deriving auspice.

Keightley, David N. *Sources of Shang History: The Oracle-Bone Inscriptions of Bronze Age China*. Berkeley: University of California Press, 1978. This was the first comprehensive study in English on the oracle bone inscriptions.

Wong, Eva. *Feng-Shui: The Ancient Wisdom of Harmonious Living for Modern Times*. Boston: Shambhala, 1996. Conducted by a scholar who is simultaneously a Daoist adept, this is a good introductory study of the concept and practice of *fengshui*.

Index

Page numbers in boldface type refer to figures and tables.

Analects (*Lunyu*), 8, 17
Annals of Lü Buwei (*Lüshi chunqiu*), 3–4, 74
"Appended Statements" (*Xicizhuan*), 45–46, 49–52, 56, 129
astrology: belief in, 1; and celestial bodies, 105; flying star, 102–103; horoscopic, 1, 121; *jianchu*, 121; as proto-science, 19
augury: and ancient Rome, 106; and celestial bodies, 106; and *fengshui*, 68; and the human body, 106; interpreting images or signs, 4–5, 62, 68, 105–106, 129; and writing, 106

bagua, 13. *See also* trigram
Bamboo Spindle (*tingzhuan*), 91
Big Dipper, 63, 78, 93, 100. *See also* Northern Ladle
bone cracking, 25–26, 30–31. *See also* crack-making, pyro-osteomancy
Book of Burial (*Zangshu*), 10, 65, 67–72, 74–75, 137
Book of Changes, alternative translation of *Yijing*. See *Classic of Changes*

Canon of the Great Mystery (*Taixuanjing*), 84, 86–87
Cerulean Dragon, 4, 63–64, 73
chance, 50, 94, 129–130
change, 3, 50, 52, 54–56, 62, 130
Change (*Yi*), 31, 50
changing line, 39, 39n, 40–41, 55–57, 62. *See also* old *yang*
Classic of Changes (*Yijing*), 51, 87, 89, 129. *See also* under original name, *Zhou Changes*

Classic on Rousing the Dragon (*Hanlongjing*), 68, 78
Compass School *fengshui* (*liqipai*): and daybooks, 69, 75–76; and fate-calculation, 52; and *Illuminating the Eight Houses*, 76–77; and *kanyu*, 66–67; and the Luo Writing, 17; and numerology, 79, 82; and *Yellow Emperor's Dwelling Classic*, 68. *See also* Flying Star *fengshui*
Confucius (551–479 BCE): physical features of, 109; and the practice of divination, 45–46, 62; and the Silk Manuscript commentaries, 45, 62; and the *Ten Wings* commentaries, 39; and Zi Gong, 45
conglomeration and dispersal (*jusan*), 10, 69, 74
contained note (*nayin*), 98, 98n
cosmograph (*shipan*), 18, 23, 65–67, 93, 95
crack-making, 26, **29**, 29–31, 37, 62
cumulative transformation (*leibian*), 58
Cups (*beijiao*), 91

Daoism: texts of, 10, 17–18, 69, 74; Golden Elixir sect of, 123
Dark Warrior/Turtle, 73, 100
daybooks (*rishu*), 13n, 69, 75, 119, 121–122
derivative hexagram (*zhigua*), 41, 56–57
Di, 2, 24, 33–34, 34n. *See also* Shang Di, High God
divination: belief in, 1; boards, 18, 66, 92; ceremony and ritual, 24, 26, 36, 38, 42; with coins, 5, 84, 89; definition of, 1–3; event or situation

divination (*continued*)
of, 62, 86–87, 90, 94–95; evolution of, 2, 8, 21–38, 62, 129–130; and fate, 3, 130; foundation of, 13; by image, 4–5, 20, 24, 62; and intuition, 1; by kings, 1, 3, 26–31, **29**, 37, 43, 97, 129; manuals of, 5, 31–32, 35–36, 39, 107, 118, 123; Neolithic, 21–24, 63–65, 129; by number, 1, 5, 22, 24, 39–41, 51–52, 55, 62, 77, 84, 88, 91, 94–95, 101–103, 123, 125; oldest forms of, 5, 21; and omens, 3, 31, **40**, 41–43, 47, 51, 113; and philosophy, 38, 44, 130; practice of, by Confucius, 45; and the production of signs, 3–4, 28, 106; *suanming*, 2–3; three systems of, 4; by trigram, 36; and turtles, 5, 21–24, 26, 28, 30, 34, 106, 119; *Yi*-style, 5, 61, 84–85; *zhanbu*, 2

divination, forms of: anatomical, 109–113; astral, 106–107; augury, 106–117; Bamboo Spindle, 91; *Canon of the Great Mystery*, 84, 86; *Classic of Changes*, 51, 87, 89; Compass School *fengshui*, 17, 66–69, 75–83, 103; Cups, 91; daybooks, 13n, 69, 75, 119, 121–122; Eight Characters, 91, 97–99; Eight-House system, 13n, 69, 76–77, 79, 81, **82**, 101, 103; eye-twitching, 111, **112;** fathoming characters, 113–117; Fire Pearl Collection, 60, 89–90; Flying Star astrology, 102; Flying Star *fengshui*, 103; Form School *fengshui*, 67–72, 103; Four Pillars Eight Character fate-calculation, 97–99; hemerology, 118–122; *jianchu*, 119–121, **120;** *kanyu*, 66–67; meteoromancy, 107–109; milfoil, 30–32, 35, 43, 84–90; Nine Star astrology, 99, 101–102, 105; Nine-Star *fengshui*, 102–105; numerical fate-calculation, 5, 19, 52, 91–92, 95, 97–101, 105, 107; numerical hexagrams, 84–86; numerology, 4–5, 22, 62, 67, 84–105; oneiromancy, 5, 106, 111–113; onomancy, 106; oracle bones, 2, 29, 85; ornithomancy, 4; Patriarch Lü's medicinal lots, 5, 123; physiognomy, 5, 106, 109, **111;** plastromancy, 25–26, 30; Plum Blossom Counting, 88; Purple Palace Ladle Numbers, 99–101, 110; pyro-osteomancy, 5, 25–26, 106; scapulimancy, 25, 30; Six-*Ren*, 92–95; Six Wands, 95–97; sortilege, 118–128; sorting sticks, 122–128; stalk-counting, 5, 45, 54, 62, 84; *Taiyi*, or the Great Unity, 99; *tongshu*, 118–119, 121; Washing for Gold, 88; Ziping, 97. See also *fengshui; fengshui,* forms of; *Zhou Changes*

dragon: as constellation, **40;** as *fengshui* topography, 68, 72–74, 78; "flying" dragon, 36; as myth and legend, 25, 119; as omen, 4; as one of the six spirits, 90; as symbol, **48;** as tomb image, 63, 65; as zodiacal animals, **19.** See also Cerulean Dragon

earth: accumulations of, 9–10; on cosmograph, 18, 92–95; formation of, 7–9; and heaven (cosmos), 3, 18, 23–25, 33, 47, 50, 66, 87, 127; and number, 52–54; patterns of, 69, 129; as phase, 11, **11,** 12, 16, **19, 78,** 82, 90, **109,** 122; protruding, 70–71; and *qi*, 8–10, 67, 69; as trigram, 14–15, 48–49, 58–59, **59,** 77, 86; veins of, 71; and water, 10, 67, 69. See also earth branches

earth branches (*dizhi*), 18, **19,** 52, 59, **59,** 88, 92–94, 98, 109, 119–120, 124

Eight Characters, 91, 97

Eight-House system, 13n, 69, 76–77, 79, 81, **82,** 101, 103

eight palaces (*bagong*), 58–59, 89

"Essentials" (*Yao*), 45, 62

eye-twitching, 111, **112**

fate, 3

fate-calculation, 5, 19, 52, 91–92, 95, 97–101, 105, 107

Index

fathoming characters (*cezi*), 106, 113–117
fengshui: and augury, 68; and auspice computation, 49; and burial, 10, 63, 65, 71; and conglomeration and dispersal, 69; and daybooks, 69, 75–76; early history of, 66–69; and five phases, 81–82; locus classicus, 70; and *luopan*, 66, **67;** and the Nine Stars, 76, 78, 100; proto-*fengshui*, 65; as proto-science, 19; residential, 65, 76
fengshui, forms of: Compass School *fengshui*, 17, 67–69, 75–83, 103; Eight-House system, 13, 76–83; Flying Star *fengshui*, 103–105; Form School *fengshui*, 10, 67, 69–75, 78; Forms and Terrain School, 66; Fujian School, 68; Intuitive School, 66; Jiangxi School, 68; Nine-Star *fengshui*, 76–83, 105; Patterns of *Qi* School, 66
Fire Pearl Collection (*Huozhulin*), 60, 89
five phases (*wuxing*): and color, 101; and the "contained note," 98; with directions and seasons, 11; and Eight-House trigrams, **82;** and the Eight Palaces, 59–60, 89; as "five elements," 11; and five "moving" stars, 11, 101, 107; and "five surnames," 68; and Guardian Stars, **78;** with heaven stems and earth branches, **19,** 94, **122;** and "inserting the stems," 89; and the Luo Writing, 77, 101–102; mutual production/generation and conquest/destruction orders, **11,** 11–13, 16, 81–82, 122; and the palace of nine halls, 15–16, **16;** and prognostication, 13; and trigram sequences, 16; and winds, 108, **109**
Flying Star divination, 102
Flying Star *fengshui* (*xuankong*), 103
Form School *fengshui* (*xingshipai*): and *Book of Burial*, 67, 69–72; and conglomeration and dispersal, 10, 69; and *Guanzi*, 67; and Prince Jin, 69; and Yang Yunsong, 68

fortune-telling, 2, 15, 94, 126
four celestial deities (*sishi*), 73
Four Pillars Eight Character fate-calculation, 97
Fujian School, 66, 68
Fuxi (legendary ruler), 34, 39, 49, 88, 129

geomancy, 5
great roving year (*dayounian*), 77, 77n, 80
Guanyin, 123–124
Guanzi, 8, 10, 67, 69
Guicang, 31–32, 35–38, 41, 43, 84, 86, 118
Guo Pu (276–324 CE), 65

heaven (*tian*): correlations with, 16, 24, 47, **48;** on cosmograph, 18, 66, 92–95; and earth (cosmos), 3, 18, 23–25, 33, 47, 50, 66, 87, 127; formation of, 7–8; mandate of, 3, 11; and number, 52–54; and *qi*, 8–10; as trigram, 14, 36, 47, **48,** 49, 58, **78;** as trigram sequence, 15–18, **15, 17,** 33, 49, 60, 77, 81–82, 88; as turtle shell, 24–25. *See also* heaven stems
heaven stems (*tiangan*), 18, **19,** 52, 59, 92, 94, 121–122, **122**
hemerology, 5, 118–119
hetu. *See* River Chart
hexagram (*gua*): *See* changing line; derivative hexagram; hexagram conversion; hexagram line; hexagram name; hexagram ruler; hexagram statement; hexagram symbol; line statements; numerical hexagrams; pure hexagrams; root hexagram; sovereign hexagrams
hexagram breaths (*guaqi*), 60
hexagram conversion, 57, 62. *See also* cumulative transformation; hexagram breaths; interlocking hexagrams; laterally linked hexagrams; line chronograms; pure hexagrams; sovereign hexagrams; waxing and waning *qi*

hexagram line, 39–40, 53, 55. *See also* line statements
hexagram name, 35, 40, 44, 46
hexagram ruler, 47, 55
hexagram statement (*guaci*), 36–37, **40**, 40–43, 47, 55–56, 58, 62, 86
"Hexagram Statement Commentary" (*Tuanzhuan*), 46–47
hexagram symbol, **14**, 35, 41, 46, **86**
High God (Shang Di), 2, 34, 34n, 94
Ho Peng Yoke, 99
horoscope, 1, 121
houtian. *See* post-heaven trigrams
Hua Tuo (c. 110–207 CE), 123

Illuminating the Eight Houses (*Bazhai mingjing*), 76
image (*xiang*): and augury, 68, 105–106; and line, 56; and number, 24, 56–57, 62; and sign, 4–5, 68, 106, 129; as trigram, 35, 49
"image and number" school, 56–57, 62
"Images Commentary" (*Xiangzhuan*), 46, 49
inserting the stems (*najia*), 59, **59**, 60, 89–90
interlocking hexagrams (*huti*), 57
Intuitive School, 66. *See also* Form School *fengshui*

jianchu, 119, **120**, 121
Jiangxi School, 66. *See also* Form School *fengshui*
Jing Fang (77–37 BCE), 56–58, 61, 89

kanyu, 66–67
Keightley, David N., 26
King Wen, 4, 39, 125

lair, 68, 72–74, 78
Laozi, 18
laterally linked hexagrams (*pangtong*), 57
Lianshan. *See* Linked Mountains
line chronograms (*yaochen*), 59, 61
line statements, **40**, 42–44, 56, 58, 62, 86, 90

Linked Mountains (*Lianshan*), 31–34
liubo. *See* Six Wands
liuren. *See* Six-Ren
Luo Writing (*luoshu*), 17, **17**, 24, 77, 82, 102
luopan, 66, **67**, 68
luoshu. *See* Luo Writing
Lü Dongbin (b. 796 CE), 123

Ma Guohan (1794–1857), 32–33, 35
magic square, 17–18, 99
mandate of heaven (*tianming*), 3, 11
Mawangdui, 35, 45, 107
"meaning and principle" school, 56
meteoromancy (*fengjiao*), 107–109
milfoil (yarrow), 5, 30–32, 35, 43, 45, 54, 62, 84–90
Mozi, 119
mutual resonance (*ganying*), 75
mythology, 7, 23–24, 25n

natal trigram (*minggua*), 77–82, **78**, 80
nayin. *See* contained note
Nine-Star astrology, 99, 101–102, 105
Nine-Star *fengshui*, 102–105
North Star (*beidouxing*), 23, 63, 65, 99–100
Northern Ladle (Beidou), 63, 100
number (*shu*): and auspice, 22, 24; and changing lines, 41, 52, 55; and choosing, 118; and image, 4, 22, 24, 62; and Luo Writing, 17, **17**, 77, 82, 101–102; and the magic square, 17–18; mystical quality of, 21, 52; odd and even, 24, 52, 61; random, 1, 5, 94–95, 123; and River Chart, **17**; school of image and number, 56–57; sequences of, 102, 118; and star spirits, 52, 77; as symbol, 41, 51; and trigram, 77, 88; and turtle spirit, 5
numerical fate-calculation (*shushu*), 5, 19, 52, 91–92, 95, 97–101, 105, 107
numerical hexagrams (*shuzigua*), 84–86
numerology, or divination by counting, 4–5, 22, 62, 67, 84–105

old *yang* (line), 41, 55–56, 89
oneiromancy, 5, 106, 111–113
onomancy, 106
oracle bones, 2, 29, 85
ornithomancy, 4

palace of nine halls (*jiugong*), 16, **16**, 68, 107
Patriarch Lü's medicinal lots, 5, 123
Patterns of *Qi* School, 66. *See also* Compass School *fengshui*
physiognomy, 5, 106, 109, **111**
plastromancy, 25–26, 30
Plum Blossom Counting (*meihuashu*), 88
post-heaven trigrams (*houtian*), **15**, 15–18, 33, 49, 60, 77, 81–82
pre-heaven trigrams (*xiantian*), 15, **15**, 49, 88
Prince Jin (Wang Ziqiao), 9–10, 69
pure hexagrams (*chun gua*), 33, 58–60
Purple Palace Ladle Numbers (*Ziwei doushu*), 99–101, 105, 110; and Western astrology, 99
pyro-osteomancy, 5, 25–26, 106

qi: assembling of, 10, 70–74; and burial, 69–74; dispersal of, 10, 60, 69, 73–74; and the earth, 67–68; and *fengshui*, 69–70; and the five phases, 11; "frozen energy," 7; and heaven, 8; natal *qi*, 77–78; and physiology, 8; primordial, 7–8; and trigrams, 16; vital *qi*, 72–73; and water, 8–10, 69–70, 73–74, 72; waxing and waning, 60; *yang/yin qi*, 60, 74, 87; and *yin* and *yang*, 8–9, 18; and Zou Yan, 11
Qi, Prince, 25, 33, 36–37
Qin Shihuangdi, 34, **34**
Qingwuzi, 69
Qu Yuan (c. 340–278 BCE), 91

Records of the Grand Historian (*Shiji*), 4, 71, 97, 107, 108, 118
rishu. *See* daybooks

River Chart (*hetu*), 17, **17**, 66
root hexagram, 55–56

scapulimancy, 25, 30
sexagesimal cycle, 18, **18**, 94, 97, 119
Shang Di, 4, 34n, 37, 94. *See also* High God
Shao Yong (1011–1077), 88
shu. *See* number
silk manuscript *Zhou Changes*, 35–36, 45
Sivin, Nathan, 87, **87**
Six-*Ren* (*liuren*), 92–95
Six Wands (*liubo*), 95–97
Smith, Richard J., 126
sortilege, 118–128
Southern Ladle, 100, 119
sovereign hexagrams (*bigua*), 60
Spring and Autumn Annals (*Chunqiu*), 30, 44, 51
stalk-counting, 5, 45, 54, 62, 84
stars, 4, 23, 63, 65, **79**, 79–82, **80**, 99–104
suanming. *See* divination

Taiyi, or the Great Unity, 99
Ten Wings, 46, 50. *See also* "Appended Statements Commentary," "Hexagram Statement Commentary," "Images Commentary," "Trigram Explanation Commentary"
tianming. *See* mandate of heaven
tiger, **19**, 42, 63–65, 73–74, 90. *See also* White Tiger
tongshu, 118–119, 121
tri-epoch (*sanyuan*). *See* great roving year
trigram (*bagua*), **14**, 14–16, 33, 35; component of hexagram, 32–33, 35–36, 46–47, 49, 58, 88–89; as image, 14, 35, 56; and numbers, 67, 77–81; sequences of, 15–16, 33, 66. *See also* natal trigram; post-heaven trigrams; pre-heaven trigrams
"Trigram Explanation Commentary" (*Shuoguazhuan*), 16, 33–34, 46–47, 49

turtle: and Dark Warrior, 73, 100; of jade, 22–24; and Luo River, 24, **25;** of myth, 24, **25;** and plastromancy, 26; for sacrifice, 22; shell boxes, 22–23; spirit, 5, 21, 24, 34
twelve animals, 121
Twelve Heavenly Generals, 95
Twelve Palaces, 99, 110, **111,** 124
Twelve Spirits, 93–94
twenty-eight lunar mansions (*ershibaxiu*), 4, 61, 73, 92–93
twenty-four seasonal breaths, 60

Vermilion Bird, 72–73

wandering soul, 58
Wang Bi (226–249), 56
Wangjiatai, 35–36, 86
Washing for Gold (*cuojin*), 88
waxing and waning *qi* (*xiaoxi*), 60
Wen Wang. *See* King Wen
White Tiger, 64, 73
wuxing. *See* five phases

xiang. *See* image
xiantian. *See* pre-heaven trigrams
Xie Shi (fl. twelfth century), 113–117
xing (form), 70.
Xu Ziping (fl. tenth century). *See* Ziping divination

Yan Kejun (1762–1843), 35
yang (male principle): as active *qi*, 9; and heaven, 8, 14, 53; as odd numbers, 61, 89; and polarity, **19,** 50, 94; and six heavenly *qi*, 8; as sunshine, 8, 65; as unbroken line, 13, 39–40, 46–47; and vital spirit, 74; as waning *qi*, 60; as young and old lines, 39, 41, 55–56, 89
Yang Xiong (53 BCE–18 CE), 86
Yang Yunsong (fl. ninth century), 68
yarrow. *See* milfoil

Yellow Emperor, 37
Yellow Emperor's Dwelling Classic (*Huangdi zhaijing*), 68
yi (change), 5, 50, 61, 84–85
Yijing. *See* *Classic of Changes*; *Zhou Changes*
yin (female principle): and bones, 74; as broken line, 13, 39–40, 46–47; and earth, 8, 14, 53; as even numbers, 61, 89; as passive *qi*, 9; and polarity, **19,** 50; as shade, 8, 65; and six heavenly *qi*, 8; as waxing *qi*, 60; as young and old lines, 39, 41, 44, 55–56, 89
Yu Fan (164–233), 56–57
Yu the Great, 10, 25

zhanbu. *See* divination
Zhou Changes (*Zhouyi*): association with Confucius, 39; commentary tradition of, 16–17, 33–34, 38, 43–51; as descendant of *Guicang*, 35; graphic images of, 13–14; and Jing Fang, 56; origin of, 39; silk manuscript version of, 35–36, 45; text of, 39–43; and Wang Bi, 56–57; and *Yi*-style divination manuals, 5, 31–32; and Zhu Xi, 55–56. *See also* *Classic of Changes*
Zhouyi. *See* *Zhou Changes*
Zhu Xi (1130–1200), 55–56, 68
Zhuan Xu (legendary ruler), 24–25, **34,** 109
Zhuangzi (fl. fourth century BCE), 10, 17, 69, 74, 127
Zhuge Liang (181–234), 95, 127
Ziping divination, 97
ziwei doushu. *See* Purple Palace Ladle Numbers
zodiac, 4, 73, 92
Zou Yan (third century BCE), 11, 13
Zuo Commentary (*Zuozhuan*), 8, 30–31, 33, 44, 55

About the Author

Stephen L. Field earned his Ph.D. in Comparative Literature from the University of Texas at Austin in 1985. He is a specialist in pre-Qin Chinese literature and an authority on early Chinese cosmology as it pertains to the ancient art of *fengshui*. His best-known works are *Tian Wen: A Chinese Book of Origins* (1985), a translation of a fourth-century BCE poem on Chinese cosmology, myth, and legend; and a study of the same poem, "Cosmos, Cosmograph, and the Inquiring Poet: New Answers to the 'Heaven Questions,'" published in *Early China* 17 (1992). On the subject of *fengshui* he has published an article entitled, "The Numerology of Nine Star *Fengshui*: A *Hetu, Luoshu* Resolution of the Mystery of Directional Auspice," in *Journal of Chinese Religion*, no. 27 (1999); and a book chapter, "In Search of Dragons: The Folk Ecology of Fengshui," in N. J. Girardot et al., *Daoism and Ecology: Ways within a Cosmic Landscape* (2001). He has written on the subject of ancient divination in "Who Told the Fortunes? The Speaker in Early Chinese Divination Records" in *Asia Major* 13, no. 2 (2000). His Web site, FengshuiGate.com, gathers popular essays he has written on various aspects of *fengshui* in addition to his translation of the earliest extant *fengshui* classic, the *Zangshu*, or *Book of Burial*. He is currently J. K. and Ingrid Lee Professor of Chinese and chair of the Department of Modern Languages and Literatures at Trinity University in San Antonio, Texas.

Production Notes for Field / ANCIENT CHINESE DIVINATION

Interior design by Rich Hendel; cover design by Santos Barbasa, Jr.

Composition by Newgen-Austin

Printing and binding by The Maple-Vail Book Manufacturing Group

Printed on 60# Text White Opaque, 426 ppi